Diary of
a Desperate Dad

Diary of
a Desperate Dad

One man's guide to
family life from 0 to 5

SAM JACKSON

First published 2014
by Elliott and Thompson Limited
27 John Street
London WC1N 2BX
www.eandtbooks.com

ISBN: 978-1-90965-386-3

Text © Sam Jackson 2014

9 8 7 6 5 4 3 2 1

A catalogue record for this book is available from the British Library.

Typeset by Marie Doherty
Printed in the UK by TJ International

To O, M and E. Thank you for giving me the amazing privilege of being your dad. And to Dad, for being the best one there could ever be.

Contents

Introduction

I clearly remember the first time my wife and I went shopping for a pregnancy test kit. We could have popped one in the basket at the supermarket, along with the bread, sausages and wine, but somehow, it didn't feel right. Instead, we made our pilgrimage to the pharmacy and tracked down those magic plastic sticks in the imaginatively named 'feminine care' aisle. At the time, I couldn't understand why they were on a 'buy one, get one free' offer. Surely, I thought, you'd only ever need one. And then I realised: if the line on that little stick turns blue, you definitely want to double-check that what it's telling you really is true. So you do another test, as the enormity of what lies ahead of you begins to dawn.

Nearly six years on from that momentous experience, I somehow find myself in possession of three children, aged from 16 months to five years old. The time between that first pregnancy test and today seems to have largely been composed of a sleep-deprived haze, and I'm still not entirely sure how my wife and I have managed to clothe, feed and care for these three kids in an even vaguely acceptable way. But so far, we're getting away with it.

If you're looking for a book from a parenting expert, put this one back on the shelf. To be honest, I reckon that whole term is pretty dubious anyway: after all, is there any child in the world who ever grows up to describe their mum or dad as an 'expert parent'? When I first discovered I was going to become a dad, I wanted to find a book that gave me a real, unvarnished understanding of what I was letting myself in for. But most of the books for new fathers that I found tended to come from the perspective of 'Woah! Your missus is pregnant! Time to stop getting drunk every night and start being a bit responsible!' There also didn't seem to be anything that offered some no-nonsense guidance about what happens once the baby's actually born. Ponderings on pregnancy are all well and good, but I wanted to know what I should be looking out for once the baby is on the scene.

So, I decided I'd write the book I wish had been around when I first became a dad. If you're about to embark on this wonderful, scary, exhilarating and, at times, infuriating journey, I hope you'll find plenty of encouragement here. The last five-and-a-bit years has been an amazingly happy time, but along the way it's been incredibly tough, too. From the lack of sleep to the lack of a social life, via the seemingly constant puking, pooing and snotty noses, there have been plenty of moments when the stress levels in our house have reached fever pitch. There have been more than a few incidents I'd rather forget (walking into the wrong delivery room during the birth of my second child would rank fairly high on that list, more of which later) and enough parenting errors to fill an entire book in their own right. But, as I look back,

I feel incredibly privileged to have somehow been allowed to become a father.

As that great dad Homer Simpson once commented, 'I won't lie to you. Fatherhood isn't easy like motherhood.' It's certainly a lot of fun, though, and one heck of an experience. Whether you're just about to begin this journey yourself, you've already started muddling through fatherhood, or you're a mum-to-be who thinks the man in your life might be in need of some moral support, I hope you'll find something here to help you. Failing that, if you're currently in a blissful, pre-birth state, imagining everything's going to be plain sailing when your baby arrives, I trust that the healthy dose of reality delivered over the next few pages doesn't ruin the entire experience for you. It *is* fun – honest...

Part I

We're Having a Baby

1. 'It's Blue'

'Fatherhood is the best thing I ever did. It changes your perspective. You can write a book, you can make a movie, you can paint a painting, but having kids is really the most extraordinary thing I have taken on.'

Brad Pitt

If you type the phrase 'Am I ready?' into Google, the results are rather eyebrow-raising. For starters, 'Am I ready to have a dog?' is evidently much more popular than 'Am I ready to buy a house?', but in the list of frequently asked questions, the most interesting one for me comes in at number two. It's something you may well be musing right now, or perhaps you asked yourself this very question around nine months or so ago. Quite simply, 'Am I ready to have a baby?'

In short, no. Of course you're not. You don't find enough time to see all your family and friends now, so how on earth are you going to manage once you add a baby into the already chaotic mix that is your life? And that's before we even get on to how irresponsible you are. Have you got a mortgage yet? How many parenting manuals have you read? For your partner's sake, do you know your way around a breast pump? Come to think of it, you're too young to have a baby. Or too old. Finally, never mind *you* – is your wife or girlfriend really ready for the enormity of having her life and body utterly transformed by the arrival of a screaming, kicking, hungry newborn? Of *course* you're not ready.

The fact is, none of us is ever truly ready to father a child. You can do all the preparation you want but it still won't mean you've passed the mythical parenting test. Increasingly, people are delaying having children until later in life because they want to try to sort out every other area of their lives before a baby arrives on the scene. That makes sense a lot of the time, but we're fooling ourselves if we think we're going to eventually be able to tick the box that says 'Fully Prepared for Fatherhood'. You can offer to look after your friends' kids for the day or perhaps have your nieces or nephews to stay for the weekend, but that's worlds away from having a tiny, newborn son or daughter in your hands – and not being able to hand them back to someone else. Only when that little miracle makes his or her appearance will you finally be able to start putting all your parenting ideas into practice. However, that certainly doesn't mean it's futile to at least try to be prepared.

With all that in mind, here are my top four things you *can* do to help you get ready for the amazing experience of becoming a dad. And the first is perhaps the most important of all…

Resist the temptation to exhibit Boring Dad-to-Be Syndrome

Chances are, you've already met Boring Dad-to-Be. Before his partner was expecting a baby, his Facebook posts would be about great nights out with his friends, funny encounters on the bus or requests to sponsor him to go on a free holiday, climbing Mount Kilimanjaro in aid of some spurious charity you've never heard of. Now, the sponsorship requests keep coming, but everything else is replaced by pictures of the scan, observations about birthing pools, photos of Mrs Boring Dad-to Be looking a bit more pregnant than she did last time and – worst of all – regular updates on how dilated she is during labour. (I genuinely once watched such an incident unfold, as it were, via Twitter. Goodness knows what the poor woman must have felt about the fact that her husband was sharing the news about what her vagina was doing with his followers – in 140 characters or less.)

The moment you discover your partner is pregnant might well be the most life-affirming, moving, tear-jerking time of your life – only to be surpassed by the day your child arrives into the world. It's something to rejoice in; but that doesn't mean you should now become one-dimensional. Plenty of your close friends and colleagues don't have children by choice, while others may want them desperately but not be able to have them. It's all too tempting to drone on about topics which may be the centre of your world, but which aren't even on the periphery of theirs.

In the whirlwind of excitement that accompanies the revelation that you're going to become a dad, the idea of parenthood can very easily become all-consuming. It's not uncommon for it to be all you and your partner end up talking about for days on end, but if it's also the sole topic of conversation with every other person in your life, there's a danger you'll end up testing their patience to the point where they avoid conversation with you, for fear that they won't be able to escape what is, essentially, a one-way discussion.

It's worth pointing out that, although the arrival of a baby will definitely change your life in the most amazing way, you're not about to become a completely different person. Too many parenting books, especially those written for dads, seem to want to perpetuate the myth that the birth of a child will result in you having absolutely no social life whatsoever. That's just not true: long-term, it's perfectly possible to be a happy, caring parent who doesn't spend all their spare time cleaning up baby sick or sterilising a set of bottles. Invest in your friendships with those who don't have kids just as much as with those who do, because after the mad hiatus that follows the birth, chances are you and your partner will be incredibly grateful to still have people in your life who remember what makes you tick.

Of course, you'd hope your friends and family would be interested in your news and lots of them will want to know more about it as the due date approaches. Just make sure that, along the way, you don't forget to ask them about how they are too. And ultimately, you should never, ever, think it normal to discuss your partner's labia with them – especially via social media.

Don't be Anti-Natal

So, you're about to become a dad, and hopefully you've worked out already that much of your life is going to change. If you're in any way organised or responsible, you might have even started to read up on pregnancy and labour online. But don't let the internet act as a replacement for real, face-to-face ante-natal classes.

A few months before our son's birth, my wife and I nervously went along to our very first ante-natal session. I'm reliably informed by some of my friends that their ante-natal debut was akin to some kind of spa day, filled with lovely facilities, delicious snacks and perfectly manicured people, presided over by a zen-like, softly-spoken midwife. Maybe that's how it works in the private sector, but on the good old NHS we made do with a small room at the GP's surgery, a friendly but firm midwife and a packet of HobNobs to share around the group. Between those four walls, we encountered a real mixture of south London life, all of us united by the fact that, in a few months' time, we might well be bumping into each other in the same delivery suite.

Ante-natal classes are a fantastic opportunity to learn about what you're actually letting yourself in for. They're also guaranteed to provide you with some memories for life, whether by making friends with the people sitting next to you or having an embarrassing experience with a fake breast. In our case, it was the latter: during the session on breastfeeding, our midwife felt compelled to talk in some detail about exactly how the baby 'attaches to the teat' (after you've heard that phrase a couple of times, it may take a little while before you're able look at your partner's breasts in the same way again). One of the nuggets of information she shared was that 'often, even if the nipple is inverted, the baby can still attach'. Then, in an act of brazen forthrightness, she enquired as to whether any of the women present had inverted nipples, even asking them to raise a hand if so. Not surprisingly, all hands remained clasped and eye contact was resolutely avoided. Not to be put off, like a conjurer in a circus the midwife then pulled the cord underneath her plastic boob, causing the fake nipple to magically invert.

Encounters like that are certainly memorable, but the ante-natal classes were also a useful time to focus on exactly what we would be going through in the labour ward. And I say 'we' quite deliberately. It's blindingly obvious that giving birth is both traumatic and exhausting for the woman whose responsibility it is to bring a new life into the world, but I don't think it's unreasonable to acknowledge that it can be draining for men too. Two of my three children have been delivered in theatre, the first by emergency caesarian and the second through the use of forceps and a ventouse (a sort of massive plunger, which looks like it should belong next to a huge toilet). During my wife's first labour, we ended up going to hospital three different times and the whole process lasted for 48 hours. I was tired, worried and hyper-emotional, and could only stand by and watch as the woman I loved went through something completely alien to her. But one of the main comforts for both of us was that our ante-natal midwife had mentioned most of these things to us in advance. At the very least, this meant we knew that what was happening wasn't in any way unusual.

Presume your partner knows best

If ever there was a time to veer towards agreeing with your other half, the period leading up the birth of your child is surely it. One of my most obvious mistakes during my wife's first pregnancy was to question her cravings. When, at the height of summer, she requested a large chicken pie, a packet of sausage rolls and a tin of Heinz tomato soup, I made the mistake of attempting to reason with her. I embarked on an explanation of the benefits of a more balanced diet and the importance of five fruit and veg a day for the sake of her and our unborn child. As I continued to question her sudden appetite for processed meat, she became increasingly puce with rage. Finally, at my ill-judged suggestion that perhaps she'd prefer a fresh smoothie and some grapes, she gave me one of 'those' looks (she's a teacher and can stare with the best of them) and spat through clenched teeth: 'I. JUST. NEED. SOME. PASTRY. Okay?'

I was so eager to make sure we were doing the right thing, I forgot to acknowledge that, ultimately, she knew best about her own pregnancy. All too often, couples coo 'WE'RE pregnant'; there's a nice sentiment there about this being something you're in together, but ultimately there's only one person carrying that baby – and if she says she needs a high-stodge ready-meal pie, she should not be challenged.

It's not just my own approach to my heavily pregnant wife that has sometimes been misguided, though. Prior to the birth of all three of our children, I've regularly been taken aback by how complete strangers reckon it's completely normal to invade her personal space. For some reason, certain people, especially female pensioners, seem to think it acceptable to approach a pregnant lady, slap their hand on her belly and declare to all within earshot that 'Oh yes, definitely a girl – you're carrying that one *very* low'. Inappropriate touching is suddenly deemed to be allowed, in a way that can be invasive and unwelcome. Be ready to remove your pregnant partner from such a situation at speed, or you may end up stuck between two very indignant women.

Reflecting back on the months leading up to the birth of my three children, I think it's fair to say that my most misguided moment of all came when I stupidly insisted on helping my wife with what, for the purposes of taste and decency, I shall simply refer to as 'the trim'. As your partner reaches the late stage of her pregnancy, she'll no longer have an unimpeded view of the area between her stomach and her toes. And if she's anything like my wife, she may well want to remain neatly trimmed – especially as any number of midwives and medics will be paying close attention to that part of her body in a matter of days. But take it from me: do not offer to assist with keeping everything neat and tidy down there. What's more, if you choose to ignore my sensible advice and put yourself forward for this task and she declines, you should just leave it at that. Under no circumstances should you insist on helping and leave her looking like she's been given a pubic haircut by a tipsy trainee hairdresser. Above all, you should certainly not end up sharing the tale at the pub later that evening (another indisputable demonstration of my inadequacies as a husband, which my wife still points out on a regular basis). Slightly delirious about the prospect of imminent fatherhood, I was chatting away to my friends about our experiences so far in the run-up to our first child's birth, and somehow found myself referring to my new-found topiary skills. In hindsight, this was never going to go down well at home, and to say that my mates were the model of *in*discretion afterwards would be an extreme form of understatement.

Avoid parental peer pressure

I have a confession to make: occasionally, I find newborn babies to be quite boring. I realise this is a terrible thing to say, as someone who's been in charge of a few of them myself. But let's face it: all babies really do is eat and sleep and poo. And after the first few weeks, they don't even sleep much. Plus, whatever their parents proclaim, most children aged under six months look exactly the same. That's not to say I'm not over the moon to have my own or that I don't love them (I cried like a baby, appropriately enough, when each of my children was born). But kids only really start getting interesting from around a year onwards. Before that point, it's a pretty hard slog.

One thing all babies have in their favour, though, is that their needs are very simple. A feed, the occasional nappy change and a roof over their heads are essentially all that's required. Despite this, the marketeers would have you believe that you're at risk of being arrested for child neglect if you don't spend your hard-earned cash on a whole load of baby-related tat. It's not just the people flogging us these goods who try to get us to buy into all this: our just-pregnant friends or the new parents among us can be even worse. Those best mates who would previously sit up with you late into the night to debate politics, religion and the meaning of life now only seem to be evangelical about why Britax car seats are better than all the other ones at Halfords (despite there being a 60 per cent discount on the one you wanted to buy).

The real nadir, however, comes with the parental peer pressure that's piled upon you when choosing your baby-to-be's pushchair. In 2013, it was announced that Aston Martin had teamed up with Silver Cross to create 'the most exclusive pram in the world'. The Silver Cross Surf (Aston Martin edition) is only available in Harrods – obviously – and has all sorts of luxury features including 'air-ride suspension' and a certificate of authenticity, something that will obviously be of great use when trying to cram the thing into the boot of the car or lift it onto the bus. Further design details included to tempt the cash-rich clowns who'll buy this product are its suede-lined seat pad (how do you clean the vomit off that one?) and its fully reclining seat: factors which, according to a Silver Cross spokesman, mean 'this really is a must-have for the most fast-paced lifestyle'.

Must-have? MUST-HAVE? I'll tell you, Mr Silver Cross Spokesman, what a must-have is: nappies. Honestly, have a word with yourself.

It's an extreme, obviously, but this kind of nonsense is one of the things that made me look forward to my kids getting past the baby stage. On the day I went to collect my wife and Child Number 3 from the hospital, I nearly got a parking ticket because someone had turned up on the ward, camera in hand, to try to flog us a 'photo memory pack' there and then. Dazed and knackered, we ended up letting the woman take a load of photos, bewilderedly agreeing that yes, it would indeed be lovely to get a photo of our wedding rings entwined around our newborn's face – and of course, you're absolutely right, eighty quid is a small price to pay for such a precious memory.

Although most of us don't have the spare cash to waste a couple of grand on a pram, it's still easy to end up frittering away your hard-earned money on a whole load of other stuff. Logical as it may seem to spend £60 on a bottle steriliser, if your child ends up being entirely breast-fed for their first 12 months then there is, by definition, no need for any bottles to be sterilised. And there are plenty of things that your son or daughter won't even notice or will grow out of quickly. Harsh as this might sound, there is no point in ever buying your baby a teddy or a cuddly toy. They'll receive about 74 of them when they're born – and anyway, they'll instantly become attached to just one of them, while the remaining 73 gather dust at the end of the cot. Similarly, unless you and your partner are hermits, you won't be spending every waking hour at home on your own, so it's really not essential to buy a bouncing chair, a rocking horse, an interactive play mat, a push-around dog, multiple sets of building blocks and so on. Some babies have so many toys and other paraphernalia to keep them busy, it would take them until the age of 17 to get around to playing with them all.

Sometimes, of course, you just have to go with the flow: in the 39th week of her second pregnancy, despite our house already being overrun with soft toys, my wife purchased a huge teddy for our soon-to-be-born daughter. On the same shopping trip she also bought a single daffodil, which was on its own in a bucket outside the local florist. It was a very sad scene, apparently, which caused my wife to get a little teary; she was desperately concerned about this poor, lonely flower. That evening, much as I was tempted to question why we needed yet another teddy (let alone whether daffodils can experience emotion), I decided to simply nod in agreement.

Clearly, we all want to provide for our children and see them having fun with a variety of games and toys. Our kids change so quickly, however, that by the time your child is aged three, you may well find yourself taking bags of unused baby kit to the charity shop, questioning how it was that you ended up with all this stuff in the first place. It's the same with clothes: yes, children get covered in mud and egg and vomit (rarely all at the same time, thank goodness) and therefore need a bountiful supply of spare outfits, but when you notice that your toddler's cupboard is bigger than yours, it's time to admit you've lost all sense of proportion. The most ridiculously costly items of all, though, are shoes. You know, those tiny little things, made of such a minuscule amount of material they must surely cost just a few pence to make? On the contrary, not only is every pair over £30, but they also need replacing on a ridiculously regular basis – something I innocently failed to realise prior to having children. Apparently every child must have brand new shoes and wellies, and a failure to provide them means being offi-cially classified as an uncaring and neglectful parent.

In our commercialised, materialistic world, where sleep-deprived parents can easily be lulled into putting yet another unnecessary child-related purchase onto their credit cards, it's worth remembering that our children's needs are relatively simple, and we don't need a six-figure income to provide for them. What's more, just as all babies are strik-ingly similar, the one thing you'll discover about all prams is that, no matter how much they cost, you'll still never, ever be able to get the blasted thing to steer in the right direction when you're in a desperate hurry to get somewhere.

2. And Push...

'It's not easy to watch the person you love go through that. At one point in the middle, I had to excuse myself and take 20 seconds in the bathroom to break down, wipe my eyes, beat my chest and man up for her. There's a reason they don't let men give birth.'

James Van Der Beek

One thing I've discovered about parenting is that it's awash with code words, hidden meanings and seemingly endless medical jargon. If you think learning Mandarin is hard, try deciphering some of the maternity-speak that frequently gets bandied about. From NCT to VBAC, via the epidural and the ever-so-delightful 'sweep' (if you don't know, don't ask), becoming a dad involves having to learn some new lingo. There are the hidden questions, too, my favourite being when the midwife asks: 'And who will be your birth partner?' – roughly translated as 'Will *he* be in there with you, or will you be bringing your mum instead?'

Admittedly, as you may have noticed me hint at a little earlier, I don't exactly have an unblemished record in this area. Moments after my son was born, I got mistaken for a doctor and went along with it briefly, directing a couple of patients to some ward or other (I was in medical scrubs at the time, and a little delirious). It probably wasn't the most responsible thing to do, but it felt rather exhilarating. Then, at the birth of my first daughter, I did what every birth partner is surely prone to do, and accidentally walked in on the wrong woman in labour. In my defence, it was very early in the morning, I'd been up for hours, and all hospital delivery wards look the same. No matter where you are in the maternity unit, everything is that shade of slightly-out-of-date double cream: a sort of pale brown hue, punctuated only by the bright blue outfits worn by the midwives. If your partner is giving birth in a large hospital, there will almost certainly be a whole corridor of rooms, many of which contain women in varying degrees of labour.

On this particular occasion, I'd been up all night with my wife, trying to be as helpful as possible during the early stages of childbirth. I'd already made some basic errors: turning the dial on the TENS machine the wrong way during a contraction, so that she experienced an unwelcome electric shock instead of pain relief, was probably the low point, but we both came through that incident without permanent damage. By 6.30 a.m. we were in the delivery room, but there was a brief pause in proceedings and I needed the toilet. I wandered up the corridor in a mildly trance-like state, found the gents and afterwards shuffled back down towards the room in question. As I opened the door, I remember wondering why my wife had chosen to bring the wicker bag in the corner. I didn't even remember us owning that bag. As I closed the door behind me and put my hand on the privacy curtain, the woman I presumed was my wife let out a guttural scream as an intense contraction came. I was rather surprised: she hadn't been particularly vocal thus far, preferring instead to simply mutter under her breath in moments of pain. And then I realised: the reason she didn't sound very much like my wife was because SHE WAS SOMEONE ELSE'S WIFE.

Thankfully, my hand hadn't yet started to pull the curtain along the rail, so I was yet to be spotted by this poor woman, her midwife or, perhaps most importantly, her husband. I crept out of the room, relieved that my closing of the very squeaky door happily coincided with a very loud contraction (happily for me, at least). All was well, I thought, until I turned round and saw another midwife standing in the corridor, looking at me with puzzlement.

'Is everything okay?' she asked, eyebrow quizzically raised.

'Oh yes, um, absolutely fine,' came my suitably generic response.

'She's doing really well in there...'

At which point, I broke. 'She is, yes. Very well. But she's not my wife. Actually, I'm not sure where my wife is. I mean, I know she's in one of these rooms. But not that one. Definitely not that one.'

With a pitying look that encompassed a large helping of disdain and disbelief, she proceeded to direct me to Cubicle 7, where I decided it was best to keep a low profile for a while. The mortifying feeling of intense embarrassment is something I can still recall to this day, though I did at least manage to keep the whole tale from my wife until after she had given birth.

Clearly, then, even after the delivery of two children, I was a first-class example of how not to behave during labour.

By the time our youngest daughter arrived, however, I like to think I was a model exponent of the role, which surely qualifies me now to speak as an authority on the subject of choosing your birth partner. A quick disclaimer here, before the inevitable whinges: yes, I realise that it's the woman giving birth, and yes, of course it should ultimately be her choice as to who's in the room with her, and yes, I wholeheartedly agree that a midwife saying, 'Now then, sweetheart, I'm just going to stitch you up – there's a bit of a tear down there and your clitoris might be slightly sore for the next few weeks' isn't what any man wants to hear being said to his partner (I think I was more scarred by that experience than she was). But still, the idea of excluding fathers from such a fundamental, exciting and, yes, nerve-wracking experience is something that shouldn't be done lightly.

The world would have us believe that the birth of a baby is all soft-focus and sugar-coated. The adverts are full of grinning parents cooing over an (almost certainly) airbrushed child, breastfeeding mothers whose breasts are unfeasibly pert, and fathers with perfect teeth and bright-eyed ebullience. No one's got any baby sick on their shoulder, there's not an exhausted face in sight, and, when it comes to the delivery room, with the exception of the brilliant hospital-based documentary *One Born Every Minute*, there's very little reality on show. New dads need parenting advice to be grounded in the real world, and there's no better place for that to start than the labour ward. It's incredibly helpful to understand just a little of what your partner may be going through, and how extreme and exhausting the whole process of delivering a baby really is.

Being present at the birth of our three children has deepened my relationship with my wife. It's given me an even greater respect for her (there's nothing like witnessing someone pushing a baby out to make you reconsider your definition of extreme pain), it's helped us both to realise that we can tackle things together as a team, and it's also reminded me that there are certain times in your life when you need to stop checking Facebook and instead focus on the task in hand. (To be clear: it was me on Facebook, not her. That would have been an impressive case of multi-tasking.)

If I'd relinquished my birth partner role, I'd never be able to tell my son about the moment when, just after he'd been born, the German anaesthetist got confused over the conversion rate between pounds and kilograms and consequently told me that the boy I was holding probably weighed 'about 13 pounds'. (Bear in mind, most newborns weigh between 6 and 9 pounds – leading my wife and I to believe that we'd just created the world's most obese baby.) I'd be robbed of explaining to my first daughter about the time she was born, when Daddy nearly witnessed two women giving birth – one of whom, at least, was definitely her mum. And I'd never be able to regale my youngest with the tale of how the dodgy wheelchair with a mind of its own seriously risked her being born in the Chapel of Rest if I hadn't managed eventually to get it under control and transport my wife up the correct corridor to the maternity unit.

When discussing the impending birth with the mum-to-be in your life, let her know you understand that when it comes to talking about how dilated she is during labour, or exactly where she packed the breast pads in the hospital bag, or how painful her perineum feels after that episiotomy, she may well instinctively turn to her mother rather than you. And yes, as modern, 21st-century men who know how to cook a risotto and might even admit to having shed a little tear when watching *Toy Story 3*, we fully embrace the notion of a woman's right to choose who's in that room with her when she's in the throes of giving birth. But please: think carefully before you give a thumbs-up to her picking her mum over her man. At the time, you might both reckon it best to leave you out of the equation; in years to come, though, you'll look back and laugh together at how utterly ridiculous, amazing, terrifying and bizarre the whole process of having a baby is. And your baby, who by that point may be taller than you both, will probably thank you for it.

Of course, as much as I am evangelical about a child's father being present at its birth, it's important to emphasise that you're not a lesser kind of dad if, for whatever reason, that approach doesn't work for you and your partner. For example, if you are incredibly squeamish and the mere sight of blood means you may require hospitalisation yourself, it's probably wise to avoid the delivery unit. The birth of a child is an intensely personal experience, and if it works best for you to be a part of it from a distance as opposed to at the end of the bed, that's absolutely nothing to be ashamed of.

If you *are* present at the birth of your son or daughter, however, it's good to know of ways in which you might be useful. Every woman differs, of course, but, from being in the delivery room with my wife three times, I can say for certain that you can never be too encouraging, telling your partner in between contractions how well you think she's doing, and what a brilliant mum she's going to be when this is all over. When the contractions come, though, be prepared for her to want to shout and scream incredibly loudly, or flail around on the bed, or squeeze your hand so much you wonder whether you'll ever be able to feel your fingers again. This is not the time to start telling her anything; in that moment, she's going through an unbelievably intense experience of pain, and nothing you say is going to lessen that. On the contrary, when she's trying to focus on pushing the baby out and attempting to hear the midwife's instructions, you'll only cause confusion if you choose that moment to pipe up with some supposed pearl of wisdom.

On a purely practical front, you should be ready to ensure that your partner is kept hydrated with regular drinks of water; this is, of course, something the medical staff will be handling, but they have enough to think about and usually appreciate a dad-to-be who takes the initiative. Likewise, be prepared to rub your partner's back a lot in between contractions, and to offer to wipe her no-doubt sweaty brow as the labour process gets closer to the point of birth. It's also worth pointing out the high probability (during a vaginal delivery, at least) of your partner being sick, or not quite making it to the toilet in time. Bringing an entirely new life into the world can have a momentary effect on the ability to control bodily functions – and vomiting, especially, is far from uncommon. If this is likely to make you feel queasy, try your best to retain a sense of perspective, and don't be taken aback when it happens.

Something else I recommend the two of you should discuss together is the question of where to give birth. Well over 90 per cent of births take place in hospital – but even there you have options. Water births are apparently a wonderful way of delivering a baby; we intended to opt for this with our first child. We had our 'birth plan' all sorted, imagining a quiet, calm room, with the warm water of the birthing pool gently easing the pain of childbirth, as the underfloor lighting cast ripples on the water (yes, there really was underfloor lighting). At the last minute we had to change course as, unfortunately, one of the midwives had accidentally left the tap running a few hours before and the entire delivery unit was flooded. Much as you might imagine this to be a stressful experience, we were frankly happy to do as the medical experts suggested, follow the midwives into the delivery unit and begin the rather long process of bringing our baby son into the world. Since then, I have been assured by many friends that a water birth is a great option, and perhaps you and your partner will choose that (so long as your midwife knows how to turn a tap off). Or maybe you'll choose a home birth. The concept of delivering a baby in our one-bedroom flat never appealed (wouldn't we wake all the neighbours? What happens when the midwife needs to go to the toilet and we haven't remembered to clean it? What if the baby needs specialist care and we're miles away from the hospital?), but we have friends whose children were delivered at home, and they described it as being a very beautiful and natural experience.

If, like us, you opt for a hospital birth, it's probably wise to avoid the mistake of leaving home too early.

Perhaps unsurprisingly, when my wife went into labour with our first child, we were keen to get straight to the delivery suite. My suggestion of catching the N55 night bus ('We'll save a fortune on parking – and anyway, the contractions are still fairly mild, aren't they?') had fallen on deaf ears and, before long, we were in the car en route to the hospital. Upon arrival, it became obvious to the midwives that our baby's head was some way off from appearing, so we were shown into a small waiting room. In one corner there was a woman on all fours making terrifying noises while her partner rubbed her back; in another, there was a ridiculously loud television and an episode of the police reality series *Road Wars*. After waiting there for 45 minutes, we were eventually seen by a midwife, who told us my wife was only two centimetres dilated (it's not until a woman reaches the magic 10 centimetres that she's officially ready to push that baby out). She prescribed a warm bath at home and some wandering around the flat until the contractions had reached a stage where there might be a vague chance of our son making an appearance in the not-too-distant future – something that, in our case, didn't actually happen until over 30 hours later. In other words, it's by no means the case that most babies arrive quickly, and you should therefore be fully prepared for a marathon instead of a sprint.

It is, of course, entirely possible that you won't have complete control over where your partner gives birth. In November 2012, supermarket chain Waitrose made British history when, for the first time ever, a woman gave birth outside one of its shops. Already too heavily in labour to get to the hospital in time, Daphne Bolus relied on security guards at Waitrose's Canary Wharf store, who intrepidly used their phones to search 'how to deliver a baby' online. They evidently followed the instructions admirably: little Matthew John arrived at 6.15 p.m., just as the evening rush for bread, milk and a ready meal was in full flow. The child's middle name was given to him by his parents in honour of John Lewis, Waitrose's parent company, which begs the question of what they would have opted for if Mrs Bolus had instead been shopping in Lidl at the time.

The week after the birth of our third child, I jotted down my Top 5 Rules for Dads-to-Be. Even if you've already sat through hours of ante-natal classes and have planned your route from home to hospital with impressive detail, there are a number of important things that I'm fairly certain no one will yet have mentioned. Entirely unscientific and most definitely not verified by any expert in midwifery, these are my observations on the dos and don'ts of labour – and although they're not proven to be either wise or correct, I hope they stand you in relatively good stead for that moment when your partner tells you 'I think it's started'.

1. Make friends with the hospital car park in advance

My first two children were born at St George's in Tooting, south London. It's a hospital we came to know well, and somewhere that was relatively easy to navigate our way around. It also had a very simple parking system: turn up, park car in empty bay, go and have a baby, come back afterwards and pay for however long you've stayed. Our youngest daughter, meanwhile, was born at the Royal Surrey in Guildford – a hospital that has a parking system so convoluted it leaves you wondering whether you're ever going to make it out of pay-and-display machine purgatory. For starters, we had to cough up in advance, at a cost of 12 quid; rather inconvenient when I only had £10 of change in my wallet. After finally locating another two pounds in change on the floor of the car, I attempted to buy a ticket – from a machine that ultimately proved to be out of order. I trekked across the car park to another machine, only discovering once I reached it that you needed to remember your parking bay number in order to purchase a ticket. Needless to say, this information was not on the tip of my tongue – and when I made it back to the car, I found that the number in question was obscured by snow and ice. All the while, my daughter was busily making her way down the birth canal and my wife was convinced our third child would be born in the back of a Ford Focus C-Max.

The challenges aren't just limited to outside the building, either. Hospitals are a bit like supermarkets: just when you've worked out where everything is, they go and change the layout – simply to confuse you. After having had one child at St George's, I personally felt very relaxed about the arrival of our second. I knew the place well, and was confident I could escort my wife from the car park to the delivery unit with ease. This, however, was before the hospital's major refurbishment programme, which had taken place since our last visit. This time I found myself completely lost as I led my wife down a rabbit warren of different corridors, all of which ended in rather unhelpful signs like 'Oncology Department', 'Security' and 'Chaplain'. It was quite tempting to open the door of the third one, in the hope that we would find a vicar who was willing to pray for the angelic arrival of a midwife, but I figured that even the most dedicated minister probably wouldn't be found in his office at 5 a.m.

The moral of this particular tale of woe is: do a recce of the hospital in advance. Check the basic things – they might seem obvious now, but they can easily wrong-foot you in the early hours of the morning. When your partner is screaming for pain relief and you're trying to use the automated payment line because you stupidly spent that spare change in the car marked 'Parking for hospital – DO NOT USE', you'll wish you'd been more prepared.

2. Apply the Taxi Driver Rule

When considering if and when to make small talk with the midwife, the Taxi Driver Rule is an essential reference point. In the same way that it's clichéd and inadvisable to ask a cabbie if he's had a busy night so far or has just started his shift, so it is futile and pointless to pose similar questions to the woman who, at that moment, has most of her forearm inside your wife because she's trying to ascertain whether or not she is fully dilated.

3. Don't forget the bendy straws

Your ante-natal midwife will drum into you and your partner the importance of the 'hospital bag' which, by the time
you've reached that 37-week milestone, should be packed
and ready to be hurled into the car at a moment's notice.
In there, you'll need a first set of clothes for the baby, some
snacks, a pair of comfy pyjamas (hers, not yours) and –
here's one the midwife definitely won't tip you off about – a
bendy straw or two. Labour is thirsty work and it's quite
hard for most women to sit up when they're in the middle of a contraction. But if you have a bendy straw then
she'll be able to have a drink while still lying down. What's
more, you'll undoubtedly impress the midwives – which, in
my case, led to them giving me a sandwich and a Twix at
4.30 a.m. So, everyone's a winner.

4. What happens in the delivery suite stays in the delivery suite

It's never right to share with anyone the details of exactly
how many stitches your partner had to have after the
birth. Even with your own mother. *Especially* with your
own mother. Nor is it advisable for every man to watch the
baby's precise moment of arrival into the world. Chances
are there'll be a lot of blood, a lot of pain and a lot of noise
(although not with every woman: my wife was more prone
to whispering 'Bugger, bugger, bugger' whenever a contraction came. This always made me think of Colin Firth in
The King's Speech – not something I expected to be brought
to mind in the final throes of labour, I have to say). It's an

intense, messy, visceral experience, and not something I ever imagined having a close-up view of. The same thing applies to caesarean sections: when my son was delivered, a particularly enthusiastic junior doctor encouraged me to come and watch him being lifted out of the womb. I felt a mixture of awe and horror – mainly horror – and very nearly fell backwards into the incubator.

5. Dads *don't* have to cut the cord

Despite what other people may tell you about it being a lovely moment of bonding with your newborn child, I personally find the dad-based ritual of 'cutting the cord' a completely gross experience that should be avoided at all costs. Ask yourself: have you ever enjoyed cutting a bit of gristle? Quite. There's not much difference. You get given a big, thick pair of scissors, not dissimilar to the ones you had for cutting textiles in Year 9 Home Economics, and as you make an incision, blood fires in all directions. It's horrible. However, I appreciate some fathers love the experience of cutting the cord; if that's you, embrace the strange scissors with pride. If you're like me, though, I'd suggest you bond with your newborn by holding him or her and shedding a tear or two, rather than sawing your way through the bodily tissue that connected them to your partner's placenta a matter of moments ago.

On a related note, although I suspect this is something that only needs saying to my own mother, it simply isn't normal to keep your firstborn child's umbilical cord in a family photo album, finally throwing it away 25 years later when pressurised to do so by your husband and three adult sons.

Your partner's labour will be a scary time: it's not easy watching the person you love the most being put through so much agony, especially when we all know complications can arise at any time. I was incredibly scared when, 46 hours into labour with our son, the doctors couldn't find his heartbeat and had to rush my wife down to theatre to get him out as quickly as possible. By the time we arrived there, his heart was happily pumping away again and all was well, but the range of emotions I experienced – from amazement and wonder to the most incredible fear and anxiety – were unlike anything I'd ever felt before.

After the initial commotion of your baby's delivery, the doctors and midwives will have a whole list of important questions to tick off. For example, can the child hear? Do they have the right number of fingers and toes? Is there anything immediately apparent that could be a cause for concern? In most cases, there isn't any cause for worry, and new parents are left alone to bond with their baby. There are, however, people who don't have such a simple experience, and the remarkable work done in the Special Care Baby Unit of every major hospital is testament to this. As a parent of three healthy children, I am only too aware of how fortunate I am, having never had to face the enormity of fathering a baby whose start in life was a particularly fragile one. The vast majority of new dads are able to enjoy those precious first few hours with only their partner and their new son or daughter in the room, and this is something to be incredibly thankful for. Often, it is the moment when the significance of the last few hours truly begins to dawn. Following the birth of our son, I remember sitting, transfixed, as my little boy and my wife lay sleeping next to each other. Having experienced the noise and activity of labour, the room was now quiet, peaceful and uneventful. Our midwife had moved on to help bring another life into the world and here we were, a shiny new family of three – who, in an instant, had been upgraded from simple 'Sam and Helen' to the altogether more exciting 'The Jacksons'.

Soon after, the peaceful phase of the proceedings came to an abrupt end: my wife and son were moved to a ward where the woman in the curtained-off cubicle beside them was intent on calling everyone she had ever met to tell them about the birth of her daughter. She must have spent about three hours on the phone to her parents, her friends and, quite possibly, her bank manager, as she gave them all a blow-by-blow account of the delivery of her baby. This rather memorable character was also very keen to declare to any-one who would listen (and to plenty of people who were in no way interested) that her boobs were incredibly sore and that she had 'nipples like rockets'.

Once the midwives declare that all is well with your new-born child, there's one thing you can be sure of. Whether the birth of your son or daughter was a speedy vaginal delivery, a planned caesarean section or an altogether more complicated arrival, the hospital won't be wanting you to take up space on their wards for any longer than is necessary. After the challenge of supporting your partner through her pregnancy and labour, an entirely new set of exciting hurdles now awaits – and it's at this point that the fun really begins.

3: The World's Most Terrifying Car Journey

'I felt something impossible for me to explain in words. Then, when they took her away, it hit me. I got scared all over again and began to feel giddy. Then it came to me... I was a father.'

Nat King Cole

Although I'm by no means a flag-waving royalist, like most people I found it hard to watch the coverage of Prince George's birth in July 2013 without feeling at least a small sense of fascination and excitement. Before our future monarch arrived, all sorts of people were wittering away on rolling news channels about what he (or she) might be called, what his birth would mean for the future of the House of Windsor (answer: not much, beyond the fact that he'd one day be king), and the task the doctors and nurses would be undertaking at this precise moment in time. Of course, no one had any idea what was happening until the birth was announced, but I'm 99 per cent certain I know what Prince William was up to: practising fitting the car seat.

As any new dad will testify, the most nerve-wracking thing about the birth of your newborn is not the labour but the moment when the midwife tells you it's time to go home.

There you are, with your exhausted partner on one side and your tiny child on the other, still feeling fairly dazed and confused yourself before you even start considering how the other two are doing. The enormity of what's happened has started to dawn, as you realise your life has changed forever. Many things remain unclear and uncertain, but the one thing you can be absolutely sure of is that, despite your best intentions, fitting the car seat for the first time will take practically as long as the labour itself.

I made the mistake of not bothering to have a trial run with this particular contraption in advance of our first child's birth: it looked relatively simple and I foolishly presumed it would be easy to strap in safely. My naivety got the better of me: standing in the hospital car park with our new son squinting at his first experience of sunlight, I discovered it was almost impossible to stretch the belt around the seat. The more I panicked, the shorter the belt seemed to become. Take it from me: give yourself a head start with your baby's car seat, if only to avoid the humiliation when another new father rocks up at the car next to you and manages to swoop his newborn child into their successfully assembled one, faster than you can mutter 'Why did I throw the manual in the bin? WHY?'

As William, Kate and George left the hospital on that summer's day, the new dad applied himself so swiftly, calmly and expertly to the task in hand that it left me wondering whether he'd had a Saturday job in Mothercare as a teenager. It's stressful enough having to fit a car seat when you're on your own, let alone with the world's media scrutinising your every move and royal correspondent Nicholas Witchell providing a running commentary to anyone who'll listen. But as that new family drove away together, what I found quite comforting was that, while William may well be used to the photographers and the protocol, he couldn't have been any more prepared than you or me when it comes to how to approach those special early days of being a dad. There are, no doubt, a whole host of doctors, nannies and advisors around him, but will that always help him to react calmly when his toddler throws his food on the floor *again*? Will being second in line to the throne make it easier for him not to have a row with his wife when they've both been up all night? And will his child always behave politely with his grandpa, especially given that he's rather important, too? No chance.

Once the wretched seat is finally fitted, you can officially commence The World's Most Terrifying Car Journey, as you bring this amazing little mini-you-and-her home for the first time. In our case, The World's Most Terrifying Car Journey involved travelling up a gridlocked Tooting High Road in the searing July sunshine and, despite an average speed of ten miles per hour for the duration of the journey, I don't think I've ever gripped the steering wheel harder, so convinced was I that I was about to veer off the road or be hit by another vehicle from any and every conceivable angle. Once home, I was overcome with a weird mix of unanticipated, impulsive emotions, ranging from wanting to have a little cry on my own to needing just to go and smell my baby boy's head again And then it hits you both: you have absolutely no idea what you are doing. Not a ruddy clue.

The first few weeks after the birth of your baby are incredibly precious and yet, with so much focus on what happens before or during the baby's arrival, it's easy to feel completely unprepared for what comes afterwards. You've read books. You've even read proper parenting manuals filled with supposedly expert advice. You've followed Mumsnet on Twitter, for goodness' sake, you feel like you're on first-name terms with Gina Ford, and you've hopefully got a couple of weeks' paternity leave stretching out before you. But still the fear comes, as you realise that nothing could ever really have prepared you for the task that now lies ahead. Despite all this, what you quickly discover is that there's something wonderfully natural about being a dad – and in those early days, you have an amazing opportunity to bond with your baby and become closer to your partner than you ever thought possible.

One of the biggest challenges about being a dad – or a mum, for that matter – is the need to preserve and protect your own family time. You may well find that all your close friends or family (plus, quite possibly, a fair few people who you thought you only exchanged Christmas cards with nowadays) turn up on your doorstep expecting to coo over your newborn; and although they're largely welcome, you do also need to carve out some time for the three of you alone.

Just three days after returning from hospital with our son, a friend of ours who we hadn't seen for ages got in touch out of the blue to say he was in our area and he'd love to call by to see the baby. In the olden days (which, for the purpose of this particular point I'm making, is any time before about 2004), Facebook was an entirely alien concept. Consequently, the only people who very quickly knew about the birth of your child were your parents, your siblings and your best mates. In other words, the special individuals in your life who merited an actual 'Hello, we've had a child' phone call. These days all it takes is a quick status update and, before you know it, all sorts of other friends-of-friends, work colleagues and that person you sat next to in History GCSE are sending you messages of congratulation or inviting themselves over to your house, at a time when your wife is still recovering from labour and your baby's life can still be measured in hours rather than days.

When our friend arrived, we naively thought he'd stay for about an hour, make the usual obligatory noises about how lovely our son was and then go home. Instead, at 11 p.m., he was still there, drinking our wine and eating our food (I can still remember the searing injustice I felt about having to cut two individual steak pies up so I could turn them into three separate portions). My wife even took to talking about the intricacies of breastfeeding quite brazenly, in the hope that this would embarrass our visitor and maybe convince him that it was time to leave. Instead, he seemed entirely unfazed and suggested we open another bottle of red.

We also had a neighbour who, upon hearing of the new arrival, took to calling by at our flat on the way home from work. Without fail she came armed with some kind of DVD box set of a dubious TV show from the 1970s or 80s, including the entire back catalogue of *The Borrowers*, which, she assured my wife, would make for perfect 'breastfeeding viewing'. Unfortunately our kindly neighbour's arrival seemed always to coincide with the ten-minute window when I'd popped out to the shops, so, every time the door-bell went, my wife would have to get off the sofa (not easy when you've just had a C-section), put the baby in one arm and gratefully accept the latest DVD donation with the other. My mother-in-law eventually put a stop to all this: when she encountered Borrowers Woman on the doorstep, she asked her kindly – but firmly, as only my mother-in-law can – to go away. I was mortified; but then I realised that if you don't prioritise your family and act in a rightfully selfish way in those first few days, you'll never get any time together. If ever there was a season for putting your family first, this is surely it.

Most new fathers are fortunate enough to be able to enjoy two weeks of paternity leave immediately after the birth of their child. Lovely as this is, it can fly by in a blur and it certainly won't feel like a holiday. Adjusting to having a baby takes much longer than a fortnight and the increasingly popular idea of shared parental leave, where the mum and dad have much more of a choice about how many weeks they each take off, is something I think we should welcome with open arms. I say 'should' quite deliberately, because this idea of taking more than two weeks off work got me wondering: what would I want to do, given the choice? Part of me says I'd jump at the chance of taking up to 52 weeks' paternity leave. After all, I absolutely love spending time with my kids and it's a constant challenge to protect that time. I remember feeling like the worst dad in the world when, unexpectedly, I once had to go in to work on my week's holiday. 'But why Daddy not take me playgroup?

Daddy said he would...' are very hard words to hear from your toddler. I was letting her down, putting an admittedly extremely important work meeting above spending time with my daughter. More time at home with the kids is the dream of a great many dads – and an awful lot of mums, too – so why wouldn't I want to have as much time off with them as possible when they're little?

At the same time, the thought of being a trailblazer for shared parental leave brings me out in a cold sweat. I love what I do for a living; if I took a year out, would I get left behind? It's certainly a fear that many women inevitably face. And anyway, so I tell myself, although the world of work is comfortable with the idea of maternity leave, what would people *think* if I said I was taking most of the year off to spend at home with my children? Then there was the whole question of what my wife would make of it all – would she like the thought of shared parental leave, or would she rather I didn't muscle in on her well-deserved time to bond with her baby?

Despite wondering how it might work in our house, I do still think it's a brilliant idea. Why should every mum be made to feel they have to stay at home, and every dad be pressurised into feeling grateful for the blink-and-you-miss-it fortnight of paternity leave? The early days you spend with your new son or daughter are an amazing time for forming relationships and learning how to be a family; it feels right to have the option of more of them, especially given that they can have a formative effect on your baby.

Recently I experienced a day that, for me, started at 5.30 a.m. By 7 a.m., I'd had to change my youngest daughter's nappy for the third time. Shortly after that, I discovered that I'd accidentally bought decaffeinated coffee the day before. It would be fair to say that my reaction to this was a little disproportionate as I furiously declared that the lack of caffeine had ruined my morning. On days like this, when you're absolutely exhausted and all you seem to be doing is wiping and cleaning and retching, it's hard to believe that your own behaviour is being understood in any kind of appreciative way by the tiny person in front of you. And yet, at some important level, even the seemingly mundane time we spend with our children in their early days, weeks and months appears to seep down into their core, providing both them and us with solid foundations for our future relationship together – and their relationship with the world around them.

If your partner is due to give birth any time soon or you've recently had a child, now's a very good time to start thinking about managing your own expectations about what life will be like with a baby in tow. By which I mean: be prepared for the house to be an absolute tip, accept that both of you will permanently smell of baby sick for a bit, and don't worry if the idea of sex slightly appals either of you for anything from a few days to a few months. Frankly, if you remember to put clothes on at all, you can count that as an achievement, let alone getting round to washing, drying or ironing anything. And when it comes to how you go about parenting, you can't go far wrong if you stay true to what you instinctively feel is the right thing to do. There are plenty of people ready to bore you senseless with their tedious views on cloth nappies versus natural ones, or breast milk versus bottles – but unless they're medical experts, feel free to ignore them wholeheartedly. My wife and I genuinely can't remember what we did for most of our son's first 12 months. The parenting just sort of happened; we got away with it, he remained intact and he's now a funny, cheeky, inquisitive five-year-old who so far seems to quite like his own parents (even if he calls me by a series of ridiculous names most of the time).

This is not to say there won't be some questionable moments in the early days. My wife's first pregnancy ended in an emergency caesarean, which was the conclusion of a long, intense and exhausting labour. As we left the hospital, emerging into the blisteringly hot day and feeling a mixture of deliriousness and panic, both of us were overwhelmed by what we had been through. In the midst of so many new experiences, a couple of days later we decided to go for a walk up the hill at the end of our road. It never even occurred to us that it wasn't generally normal to go walking barely 48 hours after such an ordeal. A local friend, who had already had three children delivered by C-section, spotted us from her car. She pulled over, gave me a stern but much-needed talking to, and practically frog-marched us home.

It may sound ridiculously naive now, but back then neither of us had a clue about what we should and shouldn't be attempting in those early days. Looking back, I wish the hospital staff had made it clearer that my wife shouldn't be doing any significant walking for at least a fortnight; we were so eager to share our beautiful son with our friends and neighbours we didn't stop to consider that, after a major operation, it really wasn't wise for her to be charging around SW12 in all weathers. Babies, incidentally, are much less complicated: if your newborn has been discharged from hospital, they are, by definition, ready to face the light of day. So long as you're able to keep your son or daughter well fed, clothed and clean, you'll find they're unlikely to complain.

Just a few weeks after the walking incident, we somehow we found ourselves in a similar situation on a five-hour car journey to north Wales. A couple of months before our son was born, we had been invited to a music festival in Caernarfon: the tickets were free, the performers were amazing, and we were going to be put up in a hotel for a couple of nights. 'What's not to love?' we thought. We were naturally aware that we would have a baby to consider; but he would surely sleep most of the time, wouldn't he? After taking about three hours to leave the house (bear in mind: this was our first experience of attempting to go anywhere with a baby for longer than an afternoon), we began the trek north. Our son screamed for nearly the whole journey. On arrival, we had 15 minutes to get changed into our finery, before heading off to what I had presumed was a dinner in a restaurant. Had I read the information more carefully (which I might have done had I not had a new baby to look after), I would have realised that we were, in fact, going to eat in a tent in an extremely muddy field. A field that was so wet due to recent rainstorms that the event had very nearly been called off.

We met the people who were hosting us in the hotel lobby. They were wearing waterproof trousers and wellies.

My wife was in an evening dress with heels; I wore a suit and smart shoes. Our coats didn't have hoods and we'd left our umbrella at home. In short, we were having a shocker – and that's before we had to sit outside, in the rain, for two hours. Amazingly, our five-week-old son *did* sleep all the way through the music, the lightning and the fireworks, something for which I will always be incredibly grateful. On our journey home, still somewhat shell-shocked by the whole experience, we tried to remember why we had never questioned our decision to take a newborn baby to a music festival in the middle of nowhere.

When it comes to some aspects of parenting, I'm a fan of the 'you've got to give everything a go' approach; not in this case, though. We expected far more of ourselves and of our son than was realistic or fair, and we vowed to pay more attention to exactly what we were being invited to in the future.

We were the first people in our group of friends to have a baby so, to some degree, we benefited from the novelty factor. Most people were sincerely interested in the minutiae of our little son's life – more so than I was, in some cases – but by the time our third child arrived, so many of our friends also had kids, no one would even bother to feign interest in her sleep patterns or the colour of her poo. Which is not something I'm in any way resentful of, I have to say.

Chances are, many of your close friends have started having kids around the same time as you and, while you always thought you were strikingly similar to them, the arrival of children may make you realise that, when it comes to some aspects of parenting, you're actually polar opposites. Perhaps you're one of those people who's decided to follow a strict regime with your baby: a two-hour sleep at precisely 1.30 p.m., feeds at pre-determined intervals, no matter how much he or she is waking the neighbours in the middle of the night, and an unbreakable rule that finger food can only consist of organic vegetables (which must be washed in Evian before consumption). In about 18 months' time, you'll reap the rewards of having a child who you can leave with a babysitter in the full knowledge that they'll sleep through until 7 o'clock the next morning, while other parents are either not going out at all or are checking their phones every five minutes for the inevitable plea to come home. But, for now, those take-life-as-it-comes parents, whom you were previously a carbon copy of in every other aspect of life, will view you as The World's Most Boring Couple. Or perhaps you and your partner have decided that you refuse to be defined entirely by your newborn. So you allow your child to stay awake until 10 p.m. after you've taken them over to the neighbours for an impromptu drink or three. Are you prepared for the unexpected look of judgement from your previously happy-go-lucky friends, whose even mild disdain at your lax child-rearing habits will knock you for six?

When our son was born we thought nothing of carting him off to all sorts of places in his portable car seat. This included one memorable evening when we were thrown out of a pub for having him with us: a rather officious barman fully enforced the 'no children after 7 p.m.' rule, even though our baby was just four weeks old and could barely be seen, sleeping by our feet. That one experience aside, the flexible bedtimes and lack of enforced routine broadly worked for us, and meant we didn't become hermits by virtue of having a small baby. As a result, we simplistically assumed it was probably the best way for everyone. So, when various friends of ours then stuck to far more of a routine, insisting their baby went to bed at exactly the same time every night, it came as something of a surprise.

It's not that one way is better than the other; every parent needs to find a setup that works best for them and their child, and you'll discover different childcare experts who advocate all sorts of approaches. But be prepared to find that, despite being very similar to your best mates in all sorts of ways, from the job you do to the football team you support, they may well end up taking a completely opposite approach to you when looking after a baby. It's something that can unexpectedly drive distance between you, which is why it's all the more important to acknowledge from the outset that there's no 'one size fits all' approach to dealing with young children. In years to come, you'll no doubt laugh with your friends about the pros and cons of your different approaches; in the meantime, don't take it personally if your best mate takes a diametrically opposed stance to child-rearing.

One example is the issue of soothing a crying baby. The overarching rule is that a baby will cry because he or she is tired, hungry or needs a nappy change. Quite often, it's a combination of all three. The hunger and the dirty nappy are easy to rectify, but the question of how to handle a tired baby is one that every parent in the land will have a view on. Probably due to being inherently weak-willed, I have never been able to embrace the idea of leaving your baby to cry themselves back to sleep. According to a great many people, if your child wakes in the night but you know he or she is clean and doesn't need a feed, you should resist the temptation to go in and comfort them. Instead, leave them alone for as long as it takes and, eventually, they'll drift back to sleep.

This is all well and good, in theory, but for so many of us, it's an approach that can be extremely stressful. When our son was born, we lived in a one-bedroom flat, and it simply wasn't possible to let him cry continually from 2 a.m. onwards. Not only would this have kept us awake, it would have also been maddening for the neighbours above, below and either side of us. It's also very hard to ignore your baby's cries when you know that being picked up by one of you will usually result in them being content. Ignoring their pleas for help can feel really mean, even if it might prove effective in the long-term.

There are very good reasons for *not* taking the approach my wife and I did, though: we found, for example, that the more we cuddled our kids back to sleep, the more often they woke – and once your baby reaches toddler age, it's not at all uncommon to then find them at the foot of your bed in the morning, having clearly clambered in there at some unknown point in the night. But, now that our three children have grown beyond the baby milestones, it's encouraging to see that they are predominantly happy kids who *do* sleep through until the morning – something that leads my wife and I to conclude that our approach to their midnight tears didn't stand them in bad stead. When it comes to the arrival of your own children, however, the most important thing is for you to find an arrangement that suits your new family, largely regardless of what your parents, your in-laws or your next-door neighbours insist is best.

Given that it's impossible to fully prepare for fatherhood in advance, there are perhaps only a few essential things you need to bear in mind to try to make those precious first few weeks as stress-free as possible. For starters, don't expect too much – not just from yourself and your partner, but from your new arrival, too. It's true that tiny babies don't react to much at all; if they open their eyes, count that as a bonus. In addition, be prepared for the fact that if you're not already very well acquainted with your washing machine, you most certainly will be within hours of arriving home from the hospital. A baby's intuitive ability to be sick all over their clean outfit when you've only just dressed them knows no bounds. And also, stock up on cotton wool balls as if your life depended on it. You're not really meant to use baby wipes on newborns' bottoms, so you'll need something else with which to clean them during the seemingly never-ending stream of nappy changes.

Your new son or daughter is the most precious and fragile person you've ever set eyes upon, so having an overriding concern for their welfare in the early days is both natural and welcome. When it comes to coughs, colds and all sorts of other everyday illnesses, though, try not to let panic set in the moment you hear a sniffle. It's easy to let concern lead to an overreaction: you end up booking an emergency GP appointment because your baby is 'having trouble breathing', whereas the reality is they've got a blocked-up nose. Of course, you should never hesitate to seek medical advice if you think something might be wrong, but it's worth trying to remain relaxed when your kids inevitably pick up germs from the world around them. My golden rule is that you should never, *ever* allow yourself to run out of Calpol. I'd sooner go without bread, milk and water than discover we didn't have any of the pink nectar on a day when one of my children is under the weather; it is the cure to pretty much every run-of-the-mill illness a toddler will face.

Ultimately, the first few weeks of being a dad bring with them all sorts of challenges, excitements and first-evers. You can also look forward to the rather pathetic thrill you'll no doubt feel when an attractive woman gives you an 'Oh, how I would love a man like you' look when you're doing the weekly shop with a tiny baby strapped to your chest. But it's all a bit of a whirlwind and in a few years, the memory of your son or daughter's first 12 months will be rather hazy. And you probably still won't be able to work the wretched car seat.

Part II

It's a Dad's World

4: The Daily Grind

'Human beings are the only creatures on earth that allow their children to come back home.'

Bill Cosby

Sometimes, as a parent, it's easy to think you've got everything under control. 'Well, this isn't as tricky as people make out,' you say to yourself smugly, as your kids play happily together and you can actually see your living-room carpet, for once free from the mass of naked (and therefore slightly demonic) dolls and little pieces of feet-destroying Lego. Those rare moments of domestic bliss are what you cling to for the majority of the time because, unfortunately, any parent who tries to convince themselves that their life is anything other than hopelessly chaotic is lying through their teeth.

Since becoming a dad, I have noticed how quickly the definition of what's normal changes. Before having kids, I wouldn't have taken kindly to someone walking into the bathroom while I was sitting on the toilet. Now it is entirely commonplace for a toddler to be attempting to make a den with the loo roll while I'm trying to use it for entirely different purposes. And there was once a time, not all that long ago, when I'd think it more than a little strange to wake up with two people lying next to me in my bed. Nowadays I'm lucky if there's any space for me at all by the time it gets to 4 a.m.

When you first take on the role of being a father, you revel in these changes to your life. I remember genuinely enjoying changing my baby son's nappies: the slow, methodical process of cleaning him up and making life better for him in that moment can be a tender experience. Coldplay's Chris Martin had it spot-on when he described this process as being 'mentally cleansing … like washing dishes, but imagine if the dishes were your kids, so you really love the dishes.' Similarly, when my baby puked up on my shoulder, it was impossible to feel cross: he was a vulnerable infant, entirely dependent on us for his well-being. Fast-forward on six months, though, and most parents will admit that, after the bubble of the early days of parenting has burst, the daily grind can drive you up the wall. That's not to say fatherhood is any less amazing, but the seemingly constant bum-wiping, feeding and interrupted nights take their toll on even the most relaxed of us, to the point where you sometimes wonder if your children are ever going to get the hang of doing anything for themselves.

One friend of mine, who I'd usually describe as the epitome of easy-going, talks about what he calls The Rage: that previously undiscovered capacity for all-guns-blazing fury that can only be brought about by an unruly child. It's something you may not even know you have until the continual pestering or misbehaviour of a tiny person causes something incandescent to well up within you. Before we had kids, my wife and I talked lots about how we wanted to raise them, helping them to grow into happy, healthy, sociable people.

We read books, we listened attentively to any advice we were given, and we thought we had a fairly good chance of doing all right with the whole parenting thing. But there are some things that you simply cannot anticipate.

A friend of mine asked me the other day, 'What should you do when your toddler ignores you?' It was a pertinent question, not least because I'd spent that morning trying to reason with an extremely irritable child who had decided to disobey every reasonable request that came his way. All my attempts to engage with him led him to declare, 'I'm not listening to you ANYMORE!' I honestly left the house feeling relieved to be heading to work; not a particularly nice emotion, but one I think most parents will be able to relate to.

One of the hardest things about being a dad is seeing it go pear-shaped even when you've supposedly done the right thing. You get down on their level, you listen to them, you try to empathise (they're only little; they're tired; they don't fully understand what you're saying), yet they still don't do as the books suggest they should. On the morning in question I hadn't slept much, having been up for what seemed like half the night with Child Number Two. Child Number One woke far too early with an attitude problem that could well have resulted in him being electronically tagged if he hadn't perked up by lunchtime. The whole experience was immensely stressful and frustrating, until I remembered something an older, wiser friend with grown-up children said to me once: 'They all get there in the end.'

Often parents can place a huge amount of expectation on their children and fret about the fact that they don't behave properly all the time, or eat their whole meal, or give elderly ladies with moustaches an all-embracing cuddle as soon as they walk through the door. Sometimes you just have to accept that it doesn't always make sense. Yes, it's completely illogical that your child is getting cross and grumpy; but then the world isn't a completely logical place when you're only four.

So, to my friend who wants to know what to do when your toddler ignores you, I say: I'm not entirely sure. I'm still working it out myself. But I suspect that the moment when he or she is ignoring you is probably not the best time to reason with them, adult-style. Sometimes, even though every fibre of your being wants to shout 'I JUST DON'T UNDERSTAND HOW YOU CAN BE THIS INFURIATINGLY UNREASONABLE!', it's better to walk away, let them have their meltdown and then come back with something fun and distracting. The maddening behaviour can then be talked through a bit later, when your child has calmed down. In fact, come to think of it, that's not a bad tactic for adult relationships, too…

I saw a sign outside a pub the other day saying 'Happy Hour from 5 p.m.' and immediately thought how this couldn't be more different from what's happening in our house around that time. The two-hour window of 5 to 7 p.m. can be entertaining on occasion but often it's like a military operation involving all sorts of warring factions (you, your eldest, your other one, and maybe another child who's come round for dinner) as you battle to make your children eat what you've cooked them, have a bath without misbehaving and go to sleep contentedly. That's not to say it's impossible to achieve these aims: a few choice tactics, cleverly deployed, can create harmony in even the most manic of households.

Take, for example, the teatime battleground. I've always found that attempting to get my kids to eat their meals works so much better when I physically place myself at the table with them. Hollering instructions to 'BEHAVE!' or 'EAT THAT UP AND STOP COMPLAINING!' while you're in the middle of doing the washing up isn't nearly as effective as sitting down alongside your child and chatting together about their day, as you subtly coax spoonfuls of food into their mouth along the way. When your children are at the table, it can be so tempting to use those 15 minutes to tidy up your ridiculously messy house, but it's far better to simply accept that you can sort that out once they've gone to bed.

Bellowing instructions at them, or showing your exasperation is hardly ever effective, but it's amazing how quickly a child can eat their tea if they think it's part of a fun new game. I find that telling a toddler to 'look after my favourite mouthful' will almost certainly make them gobble up whatever you've put on their fork. Another tried-and-tested tactic in the Jackson household is placing the food in the shape of a smiley face (broccoli is clearly so much more tasty once it's become an eyebrow).

Even when applying all sorts of parenting strategies, a stressful teatime/bathtime/bedtime combo is genuinely more of a challenge for my patience than a mind-numbingly long work meeting or a difficult discussion with a colleague; and when such a challenge falls at the end of a busy day, the problem is only exacerbated. It's in this context that I share my favourite story about the daily grind of having young kids, courtesy of my friend Sam (and no, this definitely isn't a story about me, dressed up as being about someone else).

Several years ago, Sam returned from a very busy day at work to be faced with a particularly fraught kids' bathtime and bedtime routine. His wife was due to be out for the evening, so, as Sam walked through the door, she pretty much left the house immediately to head off for an all-too-rare night on the town with the girls. Sam's two kids were fairly hyper, as is the norm for a three-year-old and an 18-month-old, but he managed to get the youngest one off to sleep fairly quickly. Sam's eldest son, meanwhile, was a different matter entirely.

For the next two hours, just as Sam thought his boy had reached the Land of Nod, a little head would appear round the corner of the living-room door. He was hungry; he was thirsty; he needed a wee; he was too hot; he was too cold. Every excuse was offered until finally, well after 9 p.m., this little monkey settled down to sleep. Hungry and exhausted, Sam could at last put his dinner in the microwave and slump down in front of the telly. But the moment his buttocks hit the cushions, his son appeared yet again – and, at this point, The Rage kicked in. Muttering a few choice words to himself, Sam firmly frog-marched him back to bed.

Fast-forward to the following morning, and Sam has left for work. His son is playing happily with his train set. As Thomas and James are whizzing round the track, the boy's mum clearly hears the repeated refrain: 'Choo, choo! For f**k's sake! Choo, choo! For f**k's sake!'

The whole issue of the language you use in front of your children is an interesting and sometimes humorous one, as is the topic of what words they use to talk about adults. For quite some time it felt like most of my conversations with my eldest two kids revolved around names. In particular, not calling other people names that are completely inappropriate. This ranged from their descriptions of me (my three-year-old went through a long phase of calling out 'Have a good day at work, Farty Pants!' every single morning) through to how they talk about other relatives ('Grandad's a scallywag', 'Hello, Mrs Bumhead' – you get the picture).

It's a tough one, this: you want your kids to have fun and be able to mess around, but when their primary name for you is inspired by flatulence, you know you need to draw some boundaries. The problem, of course – as with all aspects of parenting – is that you have to practise what you preach. There's no point doing the pious get-down-on-their-level-and-explain-what's-right-and-wrong thing unless they can look at you and see someone who's behaving in the way that they should be.

Most of the time I like to think I'm a relatively polite and friendly individual, not particularly prone to anger or inappropriate language. Note my use of the word 'most'. One particular autumn afternoon was a definite exception to the norm. Everything was going so well: the whole family was enjoying hanging out together and doing various fun Saturday activities – pottering about, sorting the garden, that kind of thing. The eldest two and I headed off to the local rubbish dump at one point and even the struggle to get a cumbersome piece of old furniture out of the car on my own didn't dampen my spirits. The drive home was sunny, the air was warm, and everyone seemed to be very glass-half-full about life. Everyone except the old man in the car behind us.

As we approached our house, he hooted his horn. And then, without a pause, he did it again. And again. And again. All because I was reversing into our drive, and he wanted to continue down the road without having to wait a moment for me to park my car. Shaking his wizened fist at me, and with the look of a villain from a Roald Dahl story, he managed to make me feel both extremely angry and very indignant. I couldn't quite believe he was getting so irate about the fact that I'd arrived at my destination (what did he expect me to do? Continue to just beyond wherever he was going, so as to ensure his journey was completely unimpeded?) and, inevitably, as he beeped repeatedly, I started to verbalise some of those frustrations.

The result of all this was that my kids rejoiced in telling their mum repeatedly about 'that STUPID ARSE' on the drive home. In a remarkable show of memory, they relayed every single one of my descriptions of the septuagenarian road-rager, before proceeding to tell me how it wasn't nice to say nasty things about other people or call them names. I guess it's not all bad: it's surely sensible for your kids to see you arguing occasionally, or getting cross, or not doing the right thing. Just as they're learning about the world around them as they grow up, so we're learning how to parent as we go along – and it's healthy for them to know we're not perfect. Whether or not it's healthy for my two-year-old to know the phrase 'silly arse' is another question altogether.

One thing I believe it's important to stress is that there is genuine, deep joy to be found in the mundane nature of the daily grind. There's something very rewarding about seeing your child's enthusiastic response when you put a bowl of their favourite breakfast cereal before them, add extra bubbles to their bath or wash their favourite outfit as soon as they've worn it because you know they'll be happy to find it's clean again the following morning. At times, though, both mums and dads need to lift their gaze beyond the minutiae of day-to-day parenting, to a place where there are no breadsticks on the floor, no baby porridge in their hair and no 5 a.m. requests for CBeebies. My son turned five so quickly; meanwhile, with her quick wit and cheeky smile, our middle child is three going on eleven; and my baby girl is already well over a year old. All three have been very demanding little things, but no more so than you or I or anyone else at that age, I'm sure. And amidst the madness of life with small children, there are plenty of laugh-out-loud moments to see you through.

In our house, these often occur during our nightly tradition: a made-up story, which our kids always request before they nod off to sleep. Once, while settling my then four-year-old, I had one of those many lost-in-translation moments that occur with children. If your kids have reached toddler age already, you've been there before, no doubt: you say one thing, they hear it as another, and an entirely new phrase is then formed. On this particular occasion we'd had a fairly awful teatime, trying to eat together harmoniously as a family but ending up having to deal with all sorts of challenging behaviour from our rather tired children. Despite unambiguously declaring their love of fish fingers before the meal, on being served their dinner they unanimously decided they wanted pasta after all. When it quickly became clear that their parents were not going to acquiesce to their demands, they behaved as though we had suggested they eat frog spawn. Our approach, as so often in instances such as this, was to ignore their protestations until they realised there wasn't any point in making a big deal out of the supposed injustice that lay before them.

After an hour-long battle, they had finally eaten a meal. We were all exhausted so, to calm things down at the end of the day, I injected some added humour into their bedtime story, thanks to a very tall character I named 'Lanky Pants'. That got my son laughing his little head off, but what happened next made me panic about what he might share during Carpet Time at school the next day.

'Dad! That's SO funny! Wanky pants!'

Oh, good grief. Did he really just say that? 'No, LANKY Pants, with a 'luh' sound.'

'Yeah...WANKY Pants! The mouse said he was Wanky Pants because he stole his shoe! Wanky Pants!'

'LANKY.'

'The mouse called him Wanky Pants!'

Please don't let him say this at school tomorrow. PLEASE.

'He called him Lanky Pants. It means he's tall. Lanky means tall. Not...er...it's LANKY PANTS!'

And so it went on.

I'm never entirely sure what to do in those situations. Making a scene about not saying something only encourages a mischievous four-year-old to shout it from the rooftops – and I'm not convinced the neighbours would appreciate that.

Ultimately, it's all very innocent when they're little and the occasional misheard word isn't a big deal. What concerns me far more is what my kids will be saying once they reach secondary school. A work colleague of mine was recently confronted with the following comment from their daughter after school: 'Mum, is c**t a rude word?' In that light, Wanky Pants could perhaps be described as a term of endearment.

By the time you eventually get your children off to sleep, it can be tempting simply to crawl into bed yourself and gear up for another demanding day as a parent. When you have a newborn who wakes every few hours for feeding, cleaning and cuddling, the concept of an evening off is a completely alien one anyway; and when they're a few years older, you can easily find yourself spending your evenings clearing up the inevitable detritus and attempting to put all the toys back in the correct place. (My tip: buy one big toy box, and lump everything together in there. Life's way too short to worry about returning every toy, doll and puzzle piece to its original home.) Consequently, it is all too easy to lose out on quality time with your partner. To make matters worse, neither of you will probably be at your most attractive by the end of the day, either: at least one of you still has banana in your hair from teatime, and you've almost certainly got extra-large bags under your eyes from the prolonged lack of sleep. Amidst the bedlam of everyday life with children, is it still possible to foster an element of romance, excitement and intimacy? In my experience, it's feasible – but it's not without its challenges...

5: No Sex, Please, We're Parents

'My wife is a sex object. Every time I ask for sex, she objects.'

Les Dawson

'My parents had a really sweet tradition when we were growing up,' said a friend of mine one day. It was a few years ago now, and we were talking about what our respective childhoods had been like. 'Very often,' he continued, 'after my mum had finished her bath, she'd call downstairs – and my dad would go up to help dry her back.'

LONG PAUSE

'He wasn't *really* drying her back, though, was he?'

'What do you mean?'

'Well, her arms aren't particularly short, are they?'

'No, but...'

'So they were getting up to something else in the bathroom, weren't they? How often would he "dry her back"?'

'About two or three times a week...'

The look of complete horror on his face at that moment of realisation, when it became clear that his randy parents had fooled him and his siblings well into their teenage years with their bathroom charade, is something I'll never forget.

The whole issue of parents and sex tends to provoke a reaction – especially when it comes to the thought of your *own* parents (yuck, obviously). But as a sleep-deprived dad of three, the main thing I wonder in all seriousness is how, as your family grows and your kids get bigger, any parents manage to get away with it without being caught. A mate of mine recalls growing up in a house where, very often, a large wooden trunk was placed in front of his mum and dad's bedroom door every Saturday morning, preventing him and his siblings from unexpectedly running in. Subtle, it was not – but presumably very effective.

Once kids are part of the mix, finding any time for romance is quite a challenge. And nor is it always a priority, either. I remember a mum friend of mine once saying that when asked what she wanted for her birthday, she'd replied: 'A chance to do a poo on my own.' With two under-fives in tow, her birthday wish-list no longer involved flowers, chocolates and naughty underwear: she simply wanted a moment's peace without a toddler standing barely two feet away, throwing a variety of bath toys at her. With three young kids myself, it's fair to say that long, lazy mornings in bed aren't exactly an option – so my wife and I won't be investing in a wooden trunk any time soon. But just up the road from us there's a woman who has two children with an age gap of just under 11 months between them. So it's clear that some people are at it like rabbits barely days after having a baby; which is rather commendable, I guess, as well as more than a little surprising.

For me, the most unanticipated life-change as a result of having kids has been the utter exhaustion that comes from a prolonged lack of sleep. It's not something the ante-natal classes properly prepare you for – and it can knock you for six, affecting your whole life, not just your sex life. Of course you know lots of things are going to change after you have a baby: you expect your social life to be curtailed; you (hopefully) accept that you'll be spending time tending to the needs of someone other than yourself; and it may even have begun to dawn on you that, very soon, when you want to go anywhere with your baby, it will take you about three hours to leave the house. But although you realise your sleep will be affected, the all-encompassing nature of being permanently tired isn't something most of us are in any way prepared for. Obviously I knew that kids woke early, and that the days of relaxing with a coffee and the papers on a Saturday morning would probably become a thing of the past. But I don't think I fully comprehended just how draining a lack of sleep can be. Maybe it's just that my kids have been particularly bad at sleeping through the night, but I reckon most parents-to-be are blissfully unaware of the effects of sleep deprivation. It's not just that you're up early either: as your children get beyond the baby stage, they also expect you to be fully alert at 5 a.m., ready to play a game, build a den or do some ambitious junk modelling with a random collection of egg boxes and glitter.

If you find yourself getting the 4.30 p.m. slump, take some encouragement from the fact that you're not alone. While everyone else in the office is perky and bright, even the most energetic of parents find themselves flagging. When someone suggests a drink after work, I hate to admit it but my first thought is 'Nice idea, but that would *ruin* my chances of being in bed by 9.30' – and the appeal of bed has absolutely nothing to do with sex. I reckon that dads of the world – and mums, for that matter – should unite and campaign for a daily siesta in the office. Secretly, most parents would seriously consider trading in their paternity or maternity leave for a regular afternoon nap. Annoyingly, I have a sneaking suspicion that, when my kids eventually reach an age where I need them to get up at a reasonable time, they'll finally decide they do want to have a lie-in after all, and I'll be the one urging them to get up early.

On those days when you know you definitely haven't had enough sleep (which, to be honest, is the vast majority of days in my case), you can genuinely wonder how you're going to function as a good colleague, friend, partner or husband. It's crucial to manage your own expectations at these times, and to take steps to make life as easy as possible, given the circumstances. Personally speaking, I've made it clear to my colleagues that any meetings after 4 p.m. are likely to find me drifting off into a tiredness-induced fog; they know that if they want to get anything even vaguely perceptive out of me, they're better to ask earlier in the day. It's only since becoming a dad that non-iron shirts have become so appealing: after a night spent trying to get a baby to sleep, and a day in the office trying to earn a living, the last thing any sane person wants to do is spend what small amount of free time there is left chained to an ironing board.

All this is pertinent when it comes to dads – but as any mother will tell you, sleep deprivation is likely to be even more of an issue for your partner, given that she's the one doing the feeding (even though, as my biology teacher pointed out in one particularly memorable Year 9 lesson, 'many male mammals have the potential to lactate'). A lack of sleep, combined with so much of your time together being spent changing, feeding or cleaning a young baby, can have a rather detrimental effect on physical closeness. There are definitely steps you can take to mitigate tiredness: forcing yourself go to bed at 9 p.m. at least a couple of nights a week, for example, or making sure you eat a healthy diet so that you have the energy you need to see you through the day. In reality, however, it's still the case that, until your youngest child is at least three years old, it's very possible that an unbroken night's sleep will be the exception rather than the norm.

The stereotypical man is supposedly thinking about sex permanently, not getting enough of it and wishing it could last for a little longer each time. Most new dads are permanently thinking about sleep, not getting enough of it and wishing it could last for about three times longer – preferably without being interrupted in the middle to wind the baby. Just before my wife was discharged from hospital after the birth of our first child, our lovely midwife popped her head around the privacy curtain. She explained that we should avoid having sex for at least a few weeks, and she seemed to be almost apologising for causing us such inconvenience and difficulty. In reality, having just endured a 48-hour labour that culminated in an emergency caesarean, I think my wife would have thumped me if I'd even so much as dimmed the lights and smiled at her invitingly during the two months that followed our son's birth.

It's not only women who have difficulty envisaging physical intimacy after the birth of a baby, though. During labour, my wife had gone through a major operation to remove another person from her body. She'd begun breastfeeding and had her body pushed and pulled in all sorts of directions; something that occurred not just during labour but throughout the entire pregnancy, too. To me, the whole purpose of my wife's body – her entire physicality, if you like – was now all about our tiny son. I don't think there's anything wrong with admitting that you view your wife's breasts a little differently once you've repeatedly had to grab a muslin cloth and help her wipe some puked-up milk off her chest.

Similarly, if your partner ends up being one of the many women who need to have stitches after a vaginal delivery, you don't need to be a gynaecologist to realise you should probably give that area a wide berth for some time to come. And, once a few weeks or months have passed and you're both feeling like sex might at some point be an option again, you can pretty much guarantee that your baby will wake at the exact moment that you finally locate the packet of condoms underneath the pile of babygrows in the corner of the bedroom.

Even if you're not a particularly wear-your-heart-on-your-sleeve kind of man, it's definitely worth chatting about sex post-children with your partner. If you can be clear about each other's expectations now, you'll minimise any stress or misunderstanding that might occur once the baby's actually here. To be clear: it is highly unlikely that you will have any sex at all in the weeks immediately following the birth of your child. Some people buck the trend, but most new parents are so utterly exhausted by the arrival of a new baby they cannot comprehend anything more than a mumbled 'love you' and a brief kiss goodnight. You should also be aware that when your partner is 32 weeks pregnant, with a wriggling baby inside her who keeps kicking her in the ribs, she may not feel particularly enthusiastic about sex then either. Which is hardly surprising, when you think about it.

Another tip, from the perspective of someone who didn't do this enough in the early days and wishes he did, is to compliment your partner regularly on how she looks – and not just from the neck up. The media frequently shows us images of women who have recently had children – but only in order to praise those who have 'lost their baby weight', 'got their flat tummy back' or 'beaten the bulge'. In reality, chances are your partner will have stretch marks, her stomach will look different and she may be feeling more self-conscious about the way her body appears. Unless you make a conscious effort to tell her she looks good and that she did an amazing thing in bringing this beautiful baby into the world, your relationship can end up taking on a lot of unnecessary strain.

As your children get a bit older and your sex life perks up again, one of the next challenges you'll face is how and when to discuss the whole topic of sex and reproduction with your children. You may well think this is something that should wait until your son or daughter hits double figures at least, and I wouldn't blame you for it, but, from personal experience, it won't necessarily be possible for you to wait that long. Not if your child is anything like my son, that is.

'Why do boys have balls?' is a good question. It's a

question I knew was going to be posed in some form or another before too long: our youngest two children are girls and, thankfully, neither of them has a scrotum. Even if you have a particularly unobservant child, it's hard not to notice such differences at bathtime – and one midweek evening my then-four-year-old son decided to pipe up. Admittedly the timing of the question took me slightly by surprise, which perhaps explains the answer that followed.

I don't remember what conversation, if any, I had with my parents about procreation. Frankly, I think there must be some kind of evolutionary function that ensures we banish such memories from our minds. But I knew I'd have to have an answer up my sleeve for if and when I was asked a question along those lines by one of my kids. The only problem was, I hadn't even begun to formulate that answer in my head. Hence my response to the question, which went something like this: 'Er… for the tadpoles.'

THE TADPOLES?!

Inevitably the discussion couldn't end there.

'There are tadpoles in your balls, Dad?'

Right, I can get out of this. I really can. It's easy. I'll explain it clearly and calmly; after all, it's no big deal.

'Yes! That's right! Yes!'

'Why?'

Would it be wrong to ask his mum to continue the conversation from here? Of course it would. Of COURSE it would.

'Well, it's so that… well, look at Mum – she's got a baby in her tummy, and that baby started growing when I gave her a tadpole.'

The look of utter confusion on my son's face at this point is something I shall never forget.

'You gave Mum... a tadpole?'

'Yes! And then it grew even bigger, into the baby that's in Mummy's tummy! That's lovely, isn't it! Now, do you need a hair wash tonight?'

At that moment, my son turned to his little sister, raised his eyebrows and gave me a look that clearly said: 'We're not done with this yet.'

In my head I'm a dad who's always completely at ease with his kids. I'm happy to talk to them about anything. I'll merrily discuss the menstrual cycle with my daughters (I'm sure they'll both be delighted when that wonderful day arrives), I'll maturely and supportively highlight the dangers of internet pornography to my son before he hits puberty, and I'll read up on some really good ways to share the facts of life with my kids at the appropriate time. In reality, however, things don't quite work like that. After a tough day at work and a long commute home, all my good intentions went out the window when faced with a left-field question from an inquisitive four-year-old. It's only a matter of time before the conversation with my son continues, I know – and, rather worryingly, I have a feeling he may still have some unanswered questions about that lovely moment when I handed over the tadpole to his mother.

Sometimes it feels like it's hard enough to get the washing-up done, let alone find any time to create intimacy with your partner. Once you've cleared the decks, eaten something and then attempted to wind down after a fraught day at home or work, the idea of having to then romance your other half can seem a little ridiculous, especially when neither of you has the energy even to walk up the stairs. It's still an incredibly important part of your relationship, though, and it's so important to carve out time not just to share a physical closeness, but to talk to one another about topics other than your children. Just as most of us are usually quite good at putting the car in for an annual service or making a reluctant trip to the dentist every 12 months or so, maybe it's sensible to give your relationship an annual MOT.

Ever since having children, my wife and I have tried to find at least one weekend every year when we can focus on each other, without any children in tow. Once your baby is a year old, it should be fairly straightforward to leave them with a grandparent or trusted friend for the night (so long as that friend doesn't mind getting up every other hour). A night without the children doesn't have to be in an expensive hotel: sometimes it's just as enjoyable to simply spend some time at home, enjoying the novelty of drinking a double G&T at 6 p.m., rather than forcing your toddler to eat a fish finger. If you prioritise spending some quality time together, you'll almost certainly find your sex life improves. Instead of sex being something you add to the mental to-do list at the end of an already frantic day, it's the culmination of some time spent remembering exactly what it is that you love about each other.

Ultimately, I reckon this is all about grace. The grace to accept that your partner may not want to make love to you for a few months, not because she thinks you're unattractive but because she spent most of last night feeding your child and now desperately needs to rest. The grace to see that the way in which you should be expressing love to your partner right now isn't physical, it's by supporting her at a time when she may be feeling vulnerable, self-conscious and maybe even a little afraid at the enormity of what lies ahead. And the grace to laugh together about how, 18 months ago, you'd have spent the 30 minutes before falling asleep having passionate sex, whereas now you seem to be spending it with a newborn baby over your shoulder and a breast pad stuck to your foot.

In the eye of the newborn storm, it can feel like life will never change and that you'll be spending decades getting absolutely no sleep. After your baby's first year, however, you'll almost certainly start to see the wood for the trees. My children have all been terrible sleepers, but even we noticed an improvement in their nocturnal behaviour once they reached that all-important 12-month milestone. Very small babies are likely to wake frequently and need regular feeding, but, as they morph into toddlers, they'll start sleeping more soundly. At that point, a degree of normality will hopefully return and, chances are, your sex life will become fairly similar to how it was back in those heady, child-free days – maybe even better. Every couple is different, though: some new mums find it hard to cope with the changes to their bodies, while men can find it equally challenging to accept that their partner doesn't necessarily look exactly the same as before. That's nothing to feel ashamed of; you've both gone through an incredible process together, so don't be surprised if it takes you a little longer than expected to reintroduce some intimacy into the bedroom.

A final tip: if one of your annual nights without the children involves going camping together on a beautiful summer's evening, and you then end up lending your tent to your father-in-law a few weeks afterwards, I recommend first removing the condom wrapper from the little pocket next to where you put your sleeping bag.

6: I'm Going to Count to Three...

'The fundamental defect of fathers, in our competitive society, is that they want their children to be a credit to them.'

Bertrand Russell

We have a family quotes book at home. There are all sorts of gems in there, many of which have come from the mouths of our kids over the last five years. As it happens, my favourite is probably not one of the children's comments, but my own: 'You're ACTUALLY worse than Mussolini', which I apparently said to my wife in March 2011 (although neither of us can remember the context). It's very closely followed by 'Dad – you've got lovely footprints', an astute observation made by my son when he was three. Also in the running is a remark my boy made on my 30th birthday: for some reason, he chose teatime on that day to declare to the entire extended family, 'If you marry your brother or sister, your children might only have one eye.' Not what any of us expected to hear as I cut the cake, least of all my octogenarian grandmother.

In the Jackson quotes book, you'll find various heartwarming comments that give the illusion of permanent familial harmony, as well as plenty of funny remarks that we hope our kids will enjoy reading in years to come. But in among the positive quips, our tome also includes several references to days when any attempt at discipline went decidedly downhill. Perhaps the finest example of this was our then-four-year-old son declaring: 'Daddy's completely ruined my day and I'm never going to speak to him again.' I'd put him on the naughty step for continually messing around, only to then discover he had a raging ear infection that more than accounted for his slightly erratic behaviour. Another particular favourite is 'My name is NOT Mr Underpants – it is DAD.' This was the end result of a farcical bedtime routine, during which my eldest two kids proceeded to want a story, another drink, to share a bed, me to sing them a song, me to tell them a story because they didn't like the song I was singing, and so on. After getting progressively more irate with them as the minutes ticked by, they then clearly read my mood very well by beginning some kind of football-like chant in my direction, in which their dad took on the new name of Mr Underpants, who had his own special song.

It's often the most ridiculous things that tip you over the edge as a parent. After a busy day in the office, it should just be fun to have two excitable little kids calling you a silly name. And, often, it is. But sometimes, when they're trying your patience and you can't think of how to make them stop, it can all too easily make you feel like you're dealing with a monster rather than a small child. When you realise you're snapping at your kid to 'grow up', it's time to remind yourself that he or she is only four years old and, you know, the wonderful thing about being little is that you don't have to grow up just yet.

Sometimes, though, the pressure to have a good time can only make matters worse. One summer holiday my wife and I had set up a barbecue, put up a wind-break, assembled the outdoor table and chairs next to the caravan and generally put ourselves through a right old mission, all in the name of having some Enforced Family Fun. The five of us would eat together in the Cornish sun outside the little van we were staying in, the children would laugh and play happily and we'd all have toasted marshmallows at the end. Or so the theory went.

The reality was rather different: the wind blew a gale, the kids didn't want any meat and the barbecue burned through its foil base to singe the nicely manicured lawn underneath. But the marshmallows – they were a guaranteed winner, surely? After all the other upsets, this one became non-negotiable, so when Child Number 2 decided she wouldn't even try a single toasted marshmallow, we weren't having any of it. 'You'll love it!', we cried. 'You have to taste just one!' Why did she have to? What possessed us to think this was some kind of essential ritual for every two-year-old? We'd built Marshmallow-gate into such a big issue that we ended up admonishing her for something we should have never made her do in the first place – and which, if we're honest, was more for our benefit than for hers.

The moment when each of my children was born was a heady mixture of emotions, but my overriding feeling when I held each one of them for the first time was one of absolute joy. This new creation seemed to be completely perfect: entirely dependent on me and my wife, I *almost* believed they simply wouldn't be capable of unruly behaviour in the years to come. Within what's always felt like a matter of seconds, however, all three have managed to try my patience to the most unbelievably infuriating extent. The age-old question of how and when to discipline your children is one of the most contentious topics in parenting, and over the last five years I've made enough mistakes in this area to fill an entire book in its own right, so I'm not about to claim I'm in any way an expert. Hopefully, though, by reading about some of my own woeful failings, you might get a few ideas as to what *not* to do when it comes to keeping the little people in your house in order.

Reflecting upon my various parental mishaps, here are five approaches you might like to take to avoid complete chaos with small children, ensuring *they* understand the concept of discipline – and *you* don't combust in the process:

1. Think before you threaten

It's 6 p.m. on a Sunday evening. You've no clean clothes for work tomorrow, you still haven't phoned your parents as promised, but you *have* finally managed to cook a meal for you and your family to eat, which you're confident everyone will enjoy. You sit down, feeling exhausted, but, before you can take a glug of that much-needed glass of wine, your five-year-old exclaims: 'THIS IS HORRIBLE.' Already slightly on edge, you feel your chest tighten as you tell him, 'Just *eat* it.' He repeats his charming pronouncement, only this time it's accompanied by a theatrical throw of his cutlery across the table. 'If you say that one more time,' you hear yourself saying, 'you won't get any milk at bedtime.' And then, after a theatrical pause Sir Ian McKellen would be proud of, you foolishly declare 'AND... I won't read you a story, either.'

Immediately you've created a nightmare for yourself. Chances are, your child will realise your threat is probably an empty one (you only said it because you were grumpy yourself, didn't you?) and will continue to misbehave. Then you're forced either to carry it out, creating an increasingly stressful bedtime period at the end of an already fraught day, or renege on it (as your son or daughter suspects you will), undermining your authority and making them believe that your threats aren't real and can be safely ignored.

I've learnt this one the hard way: last December, one of my girls was driving me so up the wall I'm ashamed to say I told her I was going to ring Father Christmas and tell him not to bother coming down our chimney this year. She went into a completely hysterical meltdown and it took me hours to convince her that I'd changed my mind and hadn't cancelled Christmas in our household after all. Much as it sometimes feels quite cathartic to make a grandiose threat, you should make sure, before you speak, that you're happy to follow through with it. What's more, avoid at all costs the temptation to threaten something that has a negative influence on your partner. I'm still not entirely convinced my wife has forgiven me for the time I threatened no TV after school for a week if there was one more example of bad behaviour.

In trying to make appropriate threats, parents nearly always fail if they only ever come up with the punishments in the heat of the moment. When you're at your wits' end and your child is driving you a little crazy, chances are you're far less likely to suggest a reasonable threat in proportion to the misdemeanour being committed. Having been in this situation far too many times myself, I'd recommend finding the time to decide on a few suitable punishments, at a moment when your blood pressure is no higher than normal. That way, when your previously angelic toddler decides to provide a robust demonstration of the 'terrible twos', you can call upon your back-catalogue of ideas rather than devising an unreasonable or unrealistic threat there and then. The 'naughty step' has worked well in our family (although my frequent attempts to put my wife there have always fallen on deaf ears), as has the downgrading of dessert – rather than having a chocolate mousse, the misbehaving child has to settle for a yoghurt. They still get their pudding (it's not as if we're trying to starve them, in the hope that they realise the error of their ways), but there's a direct consequence to behaving badly, which hopefully makes them less likely to play up the following day.

2. 'Give Grandma a GREAT BIG KISS!' is rarely effective

On balance, I'm quite a physical sort of person. Don't get me wrong: I'm not violent; in fact, I'm pretty sure Alan Carr could beat me in a fight. But overall I like to express affection through giving the people I know well a big hug. Not everyone appreciates this: I once went to greet a vague acquaintance with a friendly arm around the shoulder, only to be literally pushed away and told: 'I do handshakes. Always have, always will. And NOTHING else.' I remain, however, a firm believer in appropriate displays of physical affection towards those with whom you are on first name terms. (Other than people at work. That would be weird.)

Quite a few children, on the other hand, don't always want to run up to adults and enjoy any kind of embrace. Nevertheless, it's easy to foist your own version of expected behaviour onto a three-year-old and then get cross when they don't act as you'd wish. My son was barely two years old when I found myself gently berating him for not greeting his great-grandparents with a big smile, a hug and an accompanying 'Hello, Great Granny, how are you? Did you have a good journey?' Rather ridiculous, obviously, but I was too concerned about what other people might think and ended up making unreasonable demands of my child. Don't get me wrong: I'm a firm believer in instilling good manners in my kids – and I absolutely *would* expect them to behave warmly towards their close relatives. But they might just need a moment to adjust to a new situation. No one wants their children to act like feral beasts (not when there are guests in the house, at least), but it's not reasonable to expect a toddler always to resemble a shiny-faced, toothy-grinned member of the von Trapp family. If they're busy playing with their toys and can only manage a smile, consider that a success. They don't need to treat every distant relative as if they're just returned from fighting a war.

3. 'But Daddy – YOU taught me to do it…'

In my list of Top 3 Most Embarrassing Moments Ever, I would without doubt include an incident with my son and eldest daughter that occurred on a summer's day in 2013. We were in a church not far from home, where we got chatting to a very friendly man in his sixties. Out of nowhere, my little girl – who at that time was aged three – announced: 'Sometimes my daddy says he has a painful leg and when I go to rub it better he farts on my hand!' In vain, I hoped that our new pensioner friend hadn't quite understood my daughter's fledgling speaking voice, but when her older brother then clarified the precise comment in great detail, I could be left in no doubt that he fully comprehended everything that had been gleefully uttered.

In that particular situation, much as I wanted to tell my daughter off for sharing such a rude story, I had to have a word with myself instead. It's hard to discipline children for inappropriate behaviour when it was me who taught them to do it in the first place. Once kids start school, they begin a lifelong process of being influenced by all sorts of different people, and much of this influence is largely beyond our control as parents. But, before that point, they learn about how to interact with the world around them from, scarily enough, us. A sobering thought – and a reminder that I should fart on them sparingly.

4. Discipline isn't only the domain of the dad

Whether or not your family setup is a so-called 'traditional' one, it's almost certain there are adults other than you in the lives of your children. They may include a partner, grand-parents, godparents, aunts and uncles or close friends. And when it comes to disciplining your children, it's pretty important to remember that you don't need to go it alone.

When I look at my own parents, I sometimes find it astonishing that they managed to raise three kids without any of us losing an eye. Put it this way: I don't know many fathers who would think there was nothing untoward about letting their toddler play with an axe. But even though I may doubt it at times, my mum and dad both have an awful lot of experience when it comes to raising and disciplining children. When our kids were born, we made a conscious decision to let other trusted adults into their lives and to allow those people to handle some of the discipline as the months and years stretched out ahead of us. All too often, when my patience has reached its limit and my kids are driving me up the wall by refusing to eat their tea, the arrival of their grandma, uncle or auntie can transform a fractious teatime into a happy family occasion. Sadly, I don't generally have a relative waiting in the downstairs loo to appear in a novelty manner during mealtimes – but on those occasions when we *are* around other trusted people, I try to take the opportunity to let them do some of the hard work.

Admittedly that approach doesn't always quite go to plan, especially if your understanding of what constitutes good parenting differs profoundly from that of your own parents (or, worse still, that of your in-laws). If, however, you're confident that the adults you're closest to will disci-pline your children in a way you'd approve of, then I strongly advocate the occasional lie-down on the sofa with a cushion over your head while your dad attempts to get your two-year-old to finish their pasta.

5. Discipline can be positive, too

When we think about disciplining a child, it's all too easy to define this as 'telling them off'. On the basis of my three kids, though, I've seen that children learn how to behave from being praised for the good stuff just as much (if not more) as they do from being continually nagged for bad behaviour. In the madness of life, when there's barely any food in the fridge and you've still not got round to removing that horrible skid mark from the back of the toilet, it is easy to forget to reflect on the everyday goodness of your children and to tell them how well you think they're doing.

Even men who are comfortable enough with their own masculinity to enjoy watching *Call the Midwife* and regularly use aftershave balm (something that still baffles my father: 'Ridiculous. I mean, what on earth's wrong with Old Spice?') may still find it tough to tell their kids how they feel about them. It can be especially tricky for men who have had a fairly formal relationship with their own parents, and who aren't used to being affirmed verbally. Even in the 21st century, there still persists this idea that 'real men' down eight pints, play rugby and wrestle a boar to the ground before lunchtime, rather than express their emotions. To be clear, I'm not saying I think the ideal family setup is one in which everyone's constantly telling each other how great they are. But words of encouragement can speak very deeply into the life of a young child, and it's vital to start from a very young age.

Once we had a particularly busy New Year's Day, with a house full of assorted family members; I felt like I'd spent more time unloading the dishwasher than interacting with my nearest and dearest. But at bedtime my son turned to me and said: 'Dad – thank you so much for everything you've done to make today so great. It was really brilliant, wasn't it?' This completely gorgeous comment made me love him even more than I already did, and led me to realise how often I fail to tell him and his sisters how good they've been. If I'm not careful, I can find myself regularly handing out admonishments to my children without stopping to thank them for being kind, considerate or helpful. Reward the good behaviour and it will probably make a welcome return in the not-too-distant future.

Good days aside, though, there will be times when it's hard not to let the discipline, or lack of it, get you down. There will be days where you've tried so hard to get it right, only for your children to metaphorically stick two fingers up at your parenting attempts by misbehaving as if their lives depended on it. At this point, it's vital to remember: hard as it may be to believe, there is always, ALWAYS, a child who is more exasperating than your own.

Whenever I'm having a day such as this, I cast my mind back to my son's fifth birthday party. On that joy-filled occasion, I walked outside into the July sunshine to find two of his classmates throwing the contents of our entire garden at the woman next door. Footballs, birthday cake, even a medium-sized plastic rocking horse; nothing was safe from their grasp. To make matters worse, when I attempted to explain to them in no uncertain terms why they shouldn't be doing this, they turned on me instead. It wasn't a particularly pleasant experience, and was certainly more serious than most of my kids' misdemeanours – and for that, I'll always be grateful. Like me, you should, therefore, take the occasional moment to reflect on the fact that your child really isn't a complete nightmare.

(If, however, you're the parent of either of the two children in question, I'm afraid you can't apply this rule. There genuinely isn't a five-year-old in the world who's more badly behaved than your uncontrollable, somewhat terrifying son. But, on the plus side, at least he's got an admirable aim.)

7: You've Got a Friend in Me

'Some people have got advice, some people
have got horror stories. I like people that look
you in the eye and say "It's gonna be cool!"'
Russell Crowe

When we started our family, some of the most supportive
and encouraging people around us were those who didn't
have children themselves. Your friends from before you had
kids are, of course, people you want to remain very close to;
becoming a dad certainly doesn't change that. Despite this,
it is inevitable that, as you go through this enormous life
change, you also benefit from being able to lean on others
who are in the same boat as you. Much as we all try to be
understanding before we have children, it can be very difficult to fully empathise with parents of young kids if you've
never experienced that process for yourself – which is why,
as you embark upon becoming a dad, it's so important to
seek the support of other people who are also bringing up
small children.

Think back over your life and, chances are, there are a
few pivotal moments when the wheels were set in motion
for you to make friends for life. Starting school; the time
your parents dropped you off at university; turning up for
your first ever 'proper job'. For most of us, once we reach
adulthood there aren't any more enforced opportunities to

make a close bond with strangers – except, that is, when you become a parent. All of a sudden, an entirely new world of potential friendships opens up before you. It's an incredible opportunity to forge close relationships with people who will stick by you for decades to come; but it's not without its potential mishaps, too.

During the early days of parenting, so many aspects of life are challenged, and it can be disconcerting if you find it a struggle to relate as closely to your friends as you did before. For men, this can be especially tough. Although by no means exclusively, it's still the case that most of us will be going back to work before our partners. A job with a long-hours culture can become incredibly difficult when you've been up with the kids since dawn; and while it's highly likely that your partner will meet other women who she can talk to about the challenges of being a mum, it's not often the case that male colleagues can be found sharing empathetically about childcare. If, like me, you're one of the first of your friends to have children, you may find it alienating to discover that your best mates aren't able to understand your situation in the way you'd like them to.

Ante-natal classes are perhaps the adult equivalent of your first day at secondary school. Everyone's quietly sussing out the rest of the room, trying to work out who the cool kids are; we all want to know where we fit in the pecking order and who we should be spending our time getting to know. You may feel a self-imposed pressure to forge friendships with a whole load of new people; but, in my experience, so long as you have one or two mates who understand where you're coming from, you'll be fine.

My friend Sam (the one who inadvertently caused his son to swear at Thomas the Tank Engine) has three kids, all close in age to mine, and our two sons have always got on well, which has been really helpful for both of us. We also have a history of spectacular failure when trying to give the boys a fun day out, which have made for some interesting shared experiences. We once decided to take them to Legoland when my son was ill, for example: despite knowing deep down we should just call the whole thing off, we reasoned that we shouldn't let a sick child dampen our spirits. Not, at least, until he vomited all over the little train that takes you to the centre of the park, much to the disgust of our fellow passengers. On another occasion we decided it would be a good idea to treat them to a morning at the cinema. Sadly, the cartoon in question wasn't quite suitable for three-year-olds, and when a huge bird attempted to swallow the main character (a tortoise, if memory serves me correctly), my son completely freaked out. Arguably the situation wasn't helped by the fact that we were watching in 3D and the effect of the special glasses meant it felt as if *we* were going to be swallowed up, too. Clambering over an entire row of people to find the exit, holding an hysterical child who had become convinced that an enormous bird was about to eat him, is not an experience I'd wish to repeat.

About three years ago now, along with a couple of friends, I helped to start a dads and kids playgroup. It was inspired by a trip the three of us made one Saturday morning to a little place in Wimbledon, which consisted of not much more than toys, snacks and about eight fathers playing happily with their offspring. Our three boys had a great time; but it also gave the dads a chance to catch up (don't believe the myth that it's only women who like to chat). It was a fun, encouraging morning, which we thought we could replicate a little closer to home without too much bother.

So, buoyed up by what was happening up the road, our idea blossomed into a dads and kids get-together even nearer to home in a church in Balham. Once a month on a Saturday morning, the rows of chairs were replaced with sofas and newspapers for the dads, and toys and games for the kids. It was really good fun: within a few months, we had around 15 regulars and we all started to get to know each other pretty well. New friendships were formed, existing ones were cemented and our other halves appreciated the opportunity for a lie-in while we took control of the childcare. There was, however, one major challenge to this otherwise harmonious experience: the man who shall forever be remembered as Nightmare Dad.

My two friends and I are fairly relaxed people (at least, that's what I like to think). But Nightmare Dad brought our stress levels up to never-before-experienced heights. For starters, he didn't just bring one young child along: he turned up with three of them. Most of the kids were aged three and under; his brood were four, six and seven. The older ones spent most of the time zooming around on bikes that were too small for them, terrifying any toddler who happened to be in their path. The middle child kept his coat and cycle helmet on throughout – which, ironically, seemed to make him *more* reckless when in control of a vehicle.

All the while, Nightmare Dad remained blissfully unaware. While his trio of terrors was causing havoc, he'd stand at the side offering such observations as 'Looks like we need a few more bacon rolls...' (having already eaten three) or 'The coffee's running a bit low...' And then, at the end, he'd seemingly NEVER LEAVE. As we attempted to clear everything up and get home, Nightmare Dad would wander around with a sort of benign smile on his face, while his three kids continued to run amok. I'm absolutely against the idea of using any kind of violence against children but, believe me, when Nightmare Dad's two oldest kids unplugged the vacuum cleaner I was using for the third time, I was seriously tempted.

Eighteen months or so after getting this gathering underway, my family and I swapped the bright lights of SW12 for the leafy streets of Hampshire. The decision wasn't entirely informed by the fact that we'd be escaping from Nightmare Dad, but it was most definitely a bonus. Where we are now is a lovely little place: there's a great community, we're not far from the coast and at least 50 per cent of the local population still have their own teeth. But one thing that took a little while to work out was what to do with the kids at the weekend, to enable them to have fun and me to meet some other dads. Down our way, there didn't immediately appear to be so much going on. However, once you scratch beneath the surface, it's all there.

In our part of the Home Counties, it's all the rage for dads to take their kids to a Tots' Disco. I was sceptical – generally speaking, I like to avoid any kind of music-led dance experience at all costs. From secondary school onwards, I found the all-encompassing embarrassment of school discos too much to bear. University was a brief respite, when it was normal to go clubbing with the rest of the student population, but, after that, life regressed with the prospect of endless wedding discos and the enforced jollity of the work Christmas party. This is why the idea of having to partake in a disco, sober, on a Saturday morning, filled me with dread. My middle one loves it there, though, and it's been a good opportunity for me to get to know some other local fathers. But, as I explained when laying down the ground rules to my daughter: if we hear even so much as the opening bars of *Saturday Night* by Whigfield, we're doing a runner.

While playgroups, discos and the like are generally a win-win situation for all involved, it doesn't always go to plan. My friend James seems to be rather prone to disasters in this area: when we were discussing this topic a while back, he looked slightly ashen as he recalled his first attempt to do some man-to-man bonding. 'Our daughter was only a couple of months old,' he said, 'and my wife thought I should take her to a toddler group. Apparently it would be a good chance for me to meet other dads. But all the other men who were there had kids who were much older than mine – and my little girl stayed asleep, in her car seat, for two hours. So I just sat there, by myself. And then we went home.'

Two years later, James had become the father of a little boy, and he was once again sent off to go and bond with some other parents. The result? 'I was chucked out of – well, politely asked to leave – Surbiton Library, because my boy had pooed his nappy, the building had no air-conditioning, and I'd forgotten to bring the changing bag with us.' Undeterred, James has continued to attempt to build a community with other local dads, despite often falling – if not at the first hurdle then generally at the second or third. His most recent mishap involved putting his son in a sling at a playgroup, and leaning over to help his daughter do some arts and crafts. The pressure placed on the little boy as a result of him being the wrong way up for a prolonged period of time resulted in him being sick in another girl's hair – which, as you can imagine, was a delight for young and old alike.

Getting to know your fellow dads isn't just beneficial when you have a newborn: as our children have entered different phases, I've found it invaluable to be able to seek the support, solace or wisdom of other dads and mums.

Never more so is this the case than when your lovely babies suddenly become terrifying toddlers. My kids love the *Despicable Me* films – in particular, that moment in the second movie when the formerly cute yellow minions turn into maniacal purple monsters, whose crazy behaviour and fiendish expressions make you want to run a mile. Witnessing your toddler enter the 'terrible twos' phase can be a similar experience. They still have moments of utter gorgeousness, but all of a sudden you have this crazed person on your hands who throws their food across the room, bangs their fists on the floor in a fit of rage when you won't give them another chocolate, and decides to vent their new-found anger in the direction of entirely innocent members of their family. Calmly reasoning with them doesn't seem to have any effect, and when you're faced with a toddler tantrum that's come from nowhere, it can be very difficult to know how to respond. And that, for me, is where G&T Friday comes in.

One of the highlights of the last few years was when, after visiting us in our new house, some of our best friends decided to follow in our footsteps and move out of London in search of a new life in the countryside. They found a place just a couple of miles away from us – and now, every other week, we have a ritual entitled G&T Friday. For the first Friday of the month, we take our children to our friends' house, stay there for the evening drinking a very welcome amount of gin, and then return home on our own with our kids tucked up on the floor of their little mates' bedrooms, where they remain until the morning. Then, a couple of weeks later, we take our turn to host our friends, similarly returning their kids home to them at 10 o'clock the following day. G&T Friday is, quite simply, amazing. It's effectively a night out every fortnight without having to get a babysitter, and the lie-in we all enjoy once a month more than compensates for the fact that, in the intervening fortnight, we have a morning of total chaos as six children pile onto our bed, barely before dawn.

Our relationship with those friends really does sustain, uplift and encourage us: we know each other's children well and are able to truly empathise when, for whatever reason, one of us is going through a tough time as a result of a disobedient toddler or a baby who's simply refusing to sleep. If you're just about to embark on the journey of becoming a dad, I'd advise you not to spread yourself too thinly when it comes to friendships with other parents. This is only from personal experience, of course, but I've found that having a few friends with whom you can be honest, real and open is far better than attempting to build an entire network of new people who are in the same boat as you. By the time you've managed to cram in work, home life and extended family, there's precious little time to spend with your friends. It's therefore wise to devote that time to building a small number of close friendships, rather than having relatively superficial relationships with a larger number of people.

Having a family undoubtedly changes you, just as it changes your friendships – both with those who have children and those who don't. With an entirely new person on the scene who wholly relies on you and your partner for their wellbeing, it's inevitable that your focus and priorities change. You're no longer able to make plans on a whim; at times you will undoubtedly miss the freedom you had to meet up with people for a drink, or hang out in the park on a summer's afternoon as lunchtime effortlessly morphs into evening. This can put pressure on relationships with your childless friends: one of my colleagues was recently frustrated by a previously close mate who, since the birth of his child, has taken to talking 'through' the baby. In response to being asked 'How are you doing?', he'll reply (with baby in hand): 'Daddy's doing very well, isn't he?' And when the question 'Are you getting much sleep?' is posed, the inevitable reply is 'Daddy's very tired, isn't he? Because I'm a little munchkin who's awake the whole time!' After a couple of bouts of this, my colleague was seriously tempted to put on his own baby voice and say: 'Daddy's become a bit of a moron, hasn't he? He seems to have lost any ability to behave like an adult anymore! How long will this go on, do we think?' For the sake of this particular friendship, he decided to let it lie – for now.

We need to make sure we don't alienate friends from the pre-kids days just as much as we owe it to ourselves to develop friendships with the fellow parents we meet along the way. Bringing up kids is an unbelievable challenge sometimes; which is why, every once in a while, we need to remind ourselves that all dads need a mate to share the load, someone who'll declare, 'You've got a friend in me' when life with young kids has become a little tough.

8: The Myth of the 'Work–Life Balance'

'A stodgy parent is no fun at all. What a child wants and deserves is a father who is SPARKY.'

Roald Dahl

In the 1980s, life was good (in my head, at least). We ate Ricicles for breakfast, we watched *Fun House* after school, and there was absolutely no twerking to be done, anywhere. What's more, I'm pretty sure our parents had it relatively easy in terms of giving their kids some attention: when my dad returned home from work every evening, there wasn't any expectation that he would be contacted by anyone from the office. Today, however, it's all too common to have a child in one hand and a Blackberry in the other. There are emails to answer, tweets to respond to, Facebook posts to like. When that's over, don't forget Skype, Instagram and WhatsApp, and that's before you get to the good old-fashioned phone calls that still need to be made. Working 9 to 5 is a myth for most of us, so how do we ensure our children don't grow up thinking that the flashing red light on the device in our hand is more important to us than they are?

I hope you'll forgive me for a moment while I have a little rant. Whoever invented the phrase 'work-life balance' needs to be put on the naughty step. This seemingly harmless description of that supposedly all-important equilibrium between home and the office is actually rather insidious: it suggests that 'work' isn't a part of 'life', and that the only meaningful things we do therefore only occur at home. A pretty dispiriting idea, if you ask me, which risks making you feel guilty the moment you leave the house in the morning. I have a similar beef with that oft-repeated job description, 'full-time mum'. My wife doesn't stop being a mum when she goes to work; that's part of her identity, 24/7. And while we're at it, I'm a full-time dad, I'll have you know, even when I'm stuck at my desk, trying desperately to finish something important at the expense of being able to get home for bedtime. Work can be good, edifying and fun, and none of us should feel guilty if we have a job. The real challenge is not necessarily about spending more time at home, but about ensuring that the time we do have with our children is of real, unadulterated quality; something that's definitely easier said than done.

Shortly after my son's second birthday, I took a day off to look after him. Our time together mainly consisted of building towers and knocking them down, with the occasional break in proceedings to eat through the stash of Petit Filous in the fridge. My 'out of office' message was set, my colleagues knew I had the day off, but still the lure of the emails seemed impossible to resist. After 10 minutes or so of tower-building, I started replying to messages one-handedly on my phone, using the other hand to pile up the bricks. I foolishly reckoned my son thought he had my undivided attention, and that he couldn't even see me scrolling through my inbox.

How wrong I was. After humouring me for a couple of minutes, he came over, took my Blackberry from my hand and said: 'Buh-bye this', playfully throwing it across the room. I couldn't possibly be angry; he was right. 'Buh-bye this', I too declared, as I then started to build the world's best tower with *both* my hands.

For me, that moment with my son was rather sobering. I realised that unless I made a conscious decision regularly to devote my complete attention to my children, they might well grow up thinking they were only of interest to me until another email arrived. If I want my kids to know how to hold a conversation, maintain eye contact and generally function like healthy human beings, I need to be a dad who doesn't always have an electronic device in front of me, tap-tapping away to justify my existence to my colleagues. It's not just job-related, either: if you're not careful, you can drift into becoming one of those dads who's more obsessed with taking the perfect Facebook-friendly picture of your child than just having a good time with them.

One of the biggest challenges in this area is when work and home collide, often unexpectedly. A week or so before the birth of our third child, I found myself trying – and failing – to work from home. My efforts were so pathetic I ended up looking forward to going back to the office, but with snow affecting my trains and the bad weather only due to get worse during the course of the day, I concluded first-thing that I would be better off staying put. After all, I had an important presentation to write, so there was too much to do to risk getting stranded somewhere. With the eldest child at school, I thought things would be fairly quiet at home – and seeing as my wife was heavily pregnant, I really didn't relish getting 'the call' in the midst of London transport chaos.

So up I got, bright and early, ready to make a start before the kids had even had their breakfast. I was just about to get cracking when my phone went off. 'Upon advice from the local education authority, the infant school is closed today.' Right. Okay. Well, I thought, I'll quickly get him out of his uniform (those were the halcyon days when he was quite keen on school, and could often be found dressed and ready to go before 7 a.m.) and find him something else to do. Then, I can get started.

For the next two hours I sat at my computer attempting to work, with a two-year-old clambering on my shoulders and a four-year-old asking 'Can we build a snowman yet?' approximately seven times per minute. My wife then took them out for a coffee with a friend. 'Great,' I thought. 'I've got an hour and a half to get stuff done.' The front door had barely been shut for a few seconds when the phone went. It was my mum. Wanting to speak to me. Although, as 'Oh! Why aren't you at work?' was her first question, why on earth she'd called me on the home phone at 11 a.m. remains a mystery.

Once my quick chat with her was done and dusted, it was time to truly crack on. And I did finally make a small amount of progress. At lunchtime, I decided I could stop for a few minutes to build the much-requested snowman with the kids. Afterwards I attempted to take various phone calls from the office and elsewhere, all the while trying to give the impression that everything was calm and focused, and that the emails I was sending hadn't been typed with one finger. But I seriously doubt that the people on the other end of the phone could have failed to spot that I was woefully out of control and completely unable to focus properly on anything other than the small, excitable people on my lap at the time. This rather fraught experience made me realise it's almost impossible to attempt to combine work and family simultaneously. Far better to instead prioritise those precious moments at the start and end of each day, when I'm fortunate enough to often be able to spend some short but special time with my children.

This all works fine in theory; the problem arises when your kids don't necessarily want to cooperate with your carefully laid plans. One of my friends spent many months being welcomed home from work with the cry of 'NO DADDY!' as his toddler threw himself on the floor, tears rolling down his cheeks. There was no particular reason for this: the guy in question is a kind, reasonable person, and a great dad – but sometimes, no matter how hard you try, if your child isn't willing to play ball, there's a limit to what you can do. As is so often the case with bringing up kids, it's one of those moments when you have to remind yourself that they're only young. Rather than descend into a deep depression over the fact that your two-year-old has rejected you, it's far better to take it on the chin, let them have a cuddle with their mum and sit there as they gradually open up and tell you about their day.

The self-imposed guilt you can feel at not achieving this mythical work-life balance can sometimes lead you to view what you do for a living as a banned topic of discussion at home – at least, banned until the children have gone to bed. I'm not sure that's always what our kids are after, though. Over the last few years, mine have loved me telling them stories about what I do at work; you may not think your children want to hear about your day serving customers, sending emails or presiding over a courtroom (I'm hoping that at least one high court judge will read this book), but you'd probably be surprised. From around the age of three onwards, children become incredibly inquisitive: they're eager to know about the world around them, and that definitely includes what their parents do when they're not at home. We shouldn't be giving our children the impression that work is somehow a bad thing; that doesn't set them up very well for the life ahead of them.

As well as the question of how to manage to balance the demands of your professional life with your family life, protecting the free time you have with your children can also be a challenge. If, like me, you're one of those people who naturally enjoys life when it's busy, you may well end up cramming far too much into your weekends, to the detriment of your kids. Starting a family is probably the most major life change any of us ever goes through, yet somehow too many of us assume we can still accomplish exactly what we managed in the days before that tiny baby made an appearance. I've made this textbook mistake countless times, agreeing to visit this or that relative, go to what's-her-name from university's wedding, and organise the school fete. Before long, you realise there isn't any time left to simply loll about with the children and take life at their pace.

I will always remember one particular day that, for us Jacksons, was meant to embody the perfect family afternoon, but saw us trying to cram in far too much, which was a recipe for disaster. For the second day running, the fun and games had started at 6 a.m., with arguments about who *really* needed a wee the most. On this occasion, the two-year-old won the much-coveted race to the toilet, sending the four-year-old into a fit of entirely disproportionate despair. After six hours of on-the-edge behaviour from all three children, largely due to the fact we had forgotten to put their black-out blind up at bedtime (something we very much regretted when, just after 5 a.m., the eldest two charged into our bedroom shouting 'IT'S THE MORNING!'), we finally managed to bundle them all into the car and head off for lunch with my gran. And that's where it all started to go badly wrong.

Already running slightly late, we turned up at the restaurant to be greeted by a friendly waiter who smiled and rather perceptively commented, 'You must be Sam.' I confirmed his suspicions. 'Your grandmother's not here,' he continued. 'Her car won't start. She phoned to ask if you could go and pick her up.' Right, back in the car to drive the two miles to her retirement village, leaving my wife to order anything on the menu that would keep our children's primitive behaviour at bay. Ten minutes later, after battling the Sunday afternoon traffic, I'm there. But crucially, she's not. Gran's gone for a wander, it seems…

After walking around the retirement village for a bit and being given more than a few suspicious looks, I jump in the car to retrace my steps. Patience is not something my gran is blessed with in abundance; could she have given up waiting for me and decided to walk to the restaurant, despite her dodgy hip and much-needed stick? A mile and a half later, there's still no sign of her. I call my wife. Her mobile rings on the seat next to me. This is not good.

Back to the retirement village I go, by this point convinced that Gran is either stuck on her stairlift or has jumped in a car with someone who looks a little bit like me. The banging on her door and shouting through her letterbox wakes the gentleman in Flat 3, but she remains missing. I'm just about to go and ask the warden for a key (by this point, I've convinced myself that I'll have to start planning Gran's funeral in a matter of hours) when the restaurant phones. Gran has arrived – but my wife apparently has no idea how she got there.

By the time I return, the formidable octogenarian is necking a large glass of wine and recovering from what she's since revealed was a two-mile trek on foot. After berating me for not noticing her waving her umbrella from the cycle path she'd decided to walk down, we eventually tuck into lunch. All is going well until the two-year-old vomits her entire meal over herself, her mum and the floor. At this point, all I want to do is steal Gran's glass and down the remainder of its contents.

After the inevitable clean-up operation, the day continued to get ever more bizarre. I provided a shuttle service at the end of the meal to get everyone back to Gran's flat – a place

I genuinely believe may be hotter than the sun – and, after that, we had to call in on 91-year-old Auntie Jane (why did we agree to do this on the same day? WHY?). On arrival, she appeared to be watching some kind of soft porn video: a man and a woman, both topless, were lying in bed kissing, while some inoffensive piano music played in the background. We were assured it was just a home video (well, quite) from the 1970s, which featured all sorts of family members performing in a play Auntie Jane had written herself. We didn't protest any further.

Once home, teatime involved the usual kids-based carnage; we eventually got them into bed, fractious and exhausted, way later than intended. The following morning, back in the office, my colleagues and I were reflecting on our weekends and one guy, who had spent the day lounging by the fire in his local pub, mentioned to me how lovely it was that Sunday could still be a day of rest. There and then, I very nearly got him to agree that, the following Sunday, he would have my kids for 24 hours – and that he might even hang out with a few of my elderly relatives for the afternoon, too.

After days like that one, I end up feeling like my return to work has a welcome change of pace about it. It's only right to expect that, as you take on a new family identity, you should still visit your close friends and relatives: apart from anything else, once your toddler has woken at 5 a.m., had breakfast before CBeebies has even begun broadcasting and is dressed in time for the 6 a.m. news bulletin, you'll be grateful to have somewhere else to go by mid-morning. But when your job seems all-consuming and your diary is rapidly filling up with all sorts of weekend commitments, don't be afraid to occasionally batten down the hatches, be gloriously anti-social, and encourage everyone in your household to remain in their pyjamas until lunchtime. After all, we only have a few years to be able to enjoy this time with our children – and once they're older, I suspect I may well miss the experience of watching the 5 a.m. news headlines with cries of 'WHEN'S CHARLIE AND LOLA ON?' in the background.

9: Just You and Me, Kid

'It is a wise father that knows his own child.'
William Shakespeare

When our first child was very small, he was the dictionary definition of 'Mummy's boy'. I genuinely think that my son's six-month-old self viewed his own father with, at times, a remarkably mature mixture of fear, suspicion and contempt – so much so that, on the rare occasions when my wife left the two of us to our own devices, he would have a complete meltdown. The real low point came when, as my wife recently reminded me, she once received 17 missed calls from me in the space of 10 minutes, after our screaming, red-faced baby had spent nearly two hours making it abundantly clear that he really didn't want to be spending the evening with his dad. Thankfully, my two girls have often been quite the opposite; in fact, only a couple of nights ago I couldn't have been happier when my youngest screamed like a banshee with her mum at bedtime but transformed into a contented, smiling baby when I came in to rock her to sleep.

Nevertheless, it's fair to say that, more often than not, a young baby will be at their most serene in the arms of their mother. If they're being breast-fed, there's an obvious reason for this; but even if they're on the bottle, they still have an innate bond with their mum that often seems to supersede their relationship with their dad – in the early days at least.

This can leave you feeling despondent: after the emotional high of the birth and the awe-inspiring nature of those first few precious weeks, once life gets into a normal pattern it can be more than a little disheartening to discover that your baby isn't that fussed about spending much one-on-one time with you. But, in my experience, it's so important to persevere when it comes to developing and strengthening your relationship with your child.

My friend Alice is one of four girls, all of whom are very close to their dad. She has no hesitation in explaining that part of the reason for this is the effort he made to devote time to each of them on an individual basis, right through their childhood. Every year, he would set aside a day for each of his daughters, where his sole focus would be on exactly what they wanted to do. These once-a-year outings weren't the only time they spent with their father, obviously, but for Alice and her sisters they represented exciting, special occasions that, today, they each look back on and see as highly significant. I'm already trying to do this with my three children; it's a little alarming how overtly intentional you have to be to make it happen, though. Diaries can fill up so quickly that a whole year can pass in a flash without you realising that you've failed to prioritise any one-on-one time with the kids.

Another challenge faced by dads (and very often mums, too) is this: we can be so used to the busy, fast-paced nature of our working life, we sometimes forget that children generally respond best to an altogether simpler, slower approach. And we often think that quality time with your child needs to be expensive: a night away in a hotel, a meal out or a trip to Peppa Pig World (I've never quite been able to face that one – yet). Very often, however, kids just want to build a den, play a game or have a good old-fashioned play-fight. Special days somewhere exciting are, of course, great fun for young children – and often for parents, too – but they're not the be-all and end-all. I love the days we spend together as a family of five; equally precious, though, are those walks through the woods, or games in the garden, or a myriad of other moments when I can enjoy meaningful, quality time with one of my children, without the distraction of their siblings or their mum.

A friend of mine called Tim excels in the role of Fun Dad. He's one of those fathers who manages to be permanently uplifting, engaging and full of excitement – not just with his own children but with everyone else's, too. Almost as soon as my son could walk, he would giggle like a maniac when Uncle Tim chased him around the kitchen and, four years on, Tim's visits are still anticipated with glee. One word that definitely wouldn't define Tim, though, is cautious. Where other parents will fret about whether or not it's really appropriate to throw a child in the air, Tim will see it as his mission to ensure they can touch the ceiling; and if someone declares a pursuit to be 'too dangerous' for young children, a glint will appear in Tim's eye as he immediately attempts to prove them wrong. So, when a change to his working week meant Tim would no longer be in the office on Fridays, his wife was ever so slightly concerned about leaving their two children in his sole care. Would he remember to close the stair-gate, keep a close eye on them near roads and ensure they didn't get some kind of playground-related injury? As a caring, understanding husband, Tim managed to convince his wife not to worry; that was, until his son scalded himself by putting his hand into a hot cup of coffee on Tim's first day in charge. Ultimately, he was absolutely fine, but the whole experience certainly led to a few heated conversations about the topic of child safety once Tim's wife arrived home from work.

We're all prone to making these kinds of mistakes, of course, which can leave you questioning your own parenting abilities. I once took my son on a walk around the woods during which I decided we should cut across a field in order to avoid the extremely waterlogged path in front of us. We'd been having a great time together, chatting away about life, the universe and whether or not his class assembly was going to go well tomorrow, when we reached a potential shortcut. Rather than attempt to use the path, I thought we should climb over the fence in front of us and make our way across a field. Lifting my son over, I let him drop down to land on his two feet on the other side. Unfortunately I hadn't realised that the seemingly robust ground below him was not just a little muddy but was, in fact, a large bog. Consequently, he disappeared almost entirely into the sludge and wailed his little head off.

Older, wiser parents, who have already been there and done that, are quick to tell you how swiftly children grow up. It is something of a cliché, similar to that moment when elderly relatives proclaim 'Haven't you GROWN!' at you in your teenage years. Like most clichés, though, there is a strong element of truth in there somewhere. Your baby will one day seem inexplicably to have turned into a toddler overnight, and when that happens their early life can feel like it's evaporating before your very eyes. Before you know it, you're waving them off on their first day at school, with a tinge of regret about how you wish you'd spent more time with them over the last few years.

Working full-time led to a funny old mix of emotions about my little boy starting school. I've only been able to drop him off a handful of times, and our first experience of this was meant to be exciting and different for us both. It didn't turn out quite like that: neither of us knew where we were going, with the result that someone from Year 5 had to lead us pityingly to my son's classroom. I'm hardly ever able to collect him at the end of the day, I don't know much about the children he's building friendships with, and, for the first time, I'm seeing him embrace a whole part of life that has very little to do with me. With just months to go until my eldest daughter starts school, I'm acutely aware of how quickly my kids are growing up. Not being there to do the walk to or from school is frustrating at times; when you add in the fact that the playground is still very much the preserve of mums, you can end up feeling that, as a dad, the whole school thing isn't anything to do with you.

There is, however, so much about our children starting school that presents some wonderful opportunities for us to develop new ways of engaging with and encouraging our children. At our son's very first parents' evening, we sat there hearing his lovely teacher chat about the six hours a day she spends with him. It was an unexpectedly moving moment. This lady seemed to know our little lad really well: she had worked out some of his personality traits, she could tell us what other children in the class thought of him, and she gave us a real boost when it came to thinking about how we parent him. She also said something that really made me stop and think. Reflecting on the kind of role models the very youngest children see before them at school, she commented: 'There are hardly ever any men. Reception teachers are all women. It's the mums who volunteer in the classroom. These children would really benefit from some male role models here, too.'

So, although work is busy, phones are permanently flashing away and there's always another email to answer, I want to make sure I don't miss the chance to have a meaningful input into this hugely important area of my children's lives. Yes, most parents' days are already very manic, but there are all sorts of options: taking one day off each term to volunteer at school, joining the governing body, even becoming the class rep for the Friends' Association. Or, at the most basic level, simply making sure to regularly ask your children plenty of engaging questions about what they get up to at school. All of this has a beneficial effect on the kids and, let's be honest, it's enjoyable for parents as well. We have a choice to make here: we can either see tasks like helping our children with their spellings as another job to add to the never-ending to-do list, or we can embrace them as opportunities to build an even closer bond. Spending 10 minutes listening to your child read before you head out of the door to work can be one of the most life-affirming ways to start the day; likewise, going to watch your child in their nativity play can bring 10 times more joy to you than it does to them.

I've been amazed to see just how different my children are when it comes to what they want from me, even though I'm pretty sure we've raised them in broadly the same way. If, like me, you live quite a time-pressured existence, with not many hours left in the day once you've factored in the commute and the day in the office, it can be tempting to hope your children respond to a 'quick-fix' form of affection. As it happens, my daughters do often fit into this camp: they're very tactile kids who respond brilliantly to being scooped up and given a cuddle; and my eldest daughter is very obviously affirmed through what we say to her. Being told 'I think you're brilliant!' often results in a big, beaming smile, and a hearty 'I love you, Dad!' in return. My son, on the other hand, is certainly an affectionate little boy, but he responds far better to being given unimpeded attention over a longer period of time. Spending an hour building a train set, constructing a Lego model or reading some stories together is his definition of contentment, as is going out on a bike ride, taking a trip to a café or playing a game of football in the park without his sisters in tow. So often, I forget this: I want him to realise I love him by virtue of the fact that I've thrown him in the air and given him a high-five at the end of a busy day; what I need to remember is that this kind of approach doesn't speak deeply to him, and I instead need regularly to carve out time for the two of us to spend together.

Parenting is a tough gig, and one that doesn't always go to plan: you can arrange a brilliant day with your children, spend some uber-quality time with them, and yet they don't necessarily appear to appreciate any of it. But it just isn't reasonable to expect to always get some kind of return on the investment of time you've made – at least, not immediately. Frequently, it's not until later in life that these formative experiences come to mind. For example, my own dad took me on some wonderful camping trips when I was little, and my recollection of these times together is remarkably vivid. The smells, sounds and sights of our weekend at a music festival in the early 1990s are as front-of-mind today as they were over 20 years ago, proving just how significant they were for me.

I don't think I ever properly expressed my gratitude at the time: instead, as soon as we returned home I was immediately back into my usual routine, bickering with my brothers, complaining about having to practise my spellings and demanding to eat my tea in front of *Gladiators*. Decades on, however, I can see that these formative experiences played a huge part in developing my relationship with my dad, creating a firm foundation of closeness that's been built upon ever since. These memories give me very real encouragement: even when my children don't seem to notice the effort I've made to cement my relationship with them, I can trust to the fact that, in years to come, they will look back and smile as they remember the times we played, chatted and laughed together.

There are clear and important reasons for spending time bonding with our children in this way. I recently read an article by psychiatrist Dr Paul Ramchandani, published in the *Journal of Child Psychology and Psychiatry*. Following a piece of research he had done, he explained that 'children tended to have greater behavioural problems when their fathers were more remote and lost in their own thoughts, or when their father interacted less with them. The association tended to be stronger for boys than for girls, suggesting that perhaps boys are more susceptible to the influence of their father from a very early age.' Just after my son's fifth birthday, I realised it had been a long while since the two of us had spent any time together one-on-one. We headed up to London on the train and, with the exception of a model of a Neanderthal woman in the Natural History Museum, which rather perturbed him, he enjoyed every minute of it. Nearly everything we did cost absolutely no money at all, save for the ice cream on the journey home – and as I tucked him into bed that night, he gave me the biggest hug imaginable and whispered in my ear: 'I think we've just had the best day ever, Dad!' Four-and-a-half years earlier, when putting him to bed on my own had involved continual crying, desperate attempts on his behalf to find a breast that, fortunately for me, wasn't there, and a huge amount of anxiety on my part, I would have found it difficult to imagine just how harmonious and rewarding this time of day could become. It's only by sticking with it and believing that things will get better that we can end up in this happy place. So, remember: you're in it for the long haul, and the eventual destination really does make the rather turbulent journey more worthwhile than you could possibly imagine.

10: Out of Office – Let the Holidays Begin

'Fatherhood is great because you can ruin someone from scratch.'

Jon Stewart

Depending on which decade you grew up in, the experiences of your early years may well be very different to mine. Anyone who is a product of the 1980s will remember when *Back to the Future* really did seem futuristic, and can probably recite the names of all four Teenage Mutant Ninja Turtles without a moment's pause. Kids of the 70s, meanwhile, may well still know the entire script of *Grease*, hark back fondly to when Space Hoppers were all the rage, and believe that the best mode of transport remains the roller skate. One common element that is part of everyone's childhood, however, and was probably being used at the very dawn of human existence, is a certain phrase that can be heard, without fail, near the start of every family holiday: 'Are we nearly there yet?'

Holidays with a young family are incredibly precious. For most of the year, you work insanely hard to juggle the various demands of life, striving to create some semblance of normality amidst the pile of breadsticks, nappy sacks and long overdue utility bills. Eventually, the supposed oasis of two weeks off arrives – but how do you ensure this is a relaxing, enjoyable time for all concerned, rather than yet another task that adds to the already high stress levels in your household?

Don't even think about leaving early

You probably consider yourself to be quite an organised person. You've planned your holiday well in advance, you or your partner have worked out exactly what you need to take with you, and you've deduced that, if you leave at 5 a.m., the journey will be a breeze, you can make it to the seaside in time for a late breakfast, and the kids will sleep in the car. Let me tell you now: the reality will be absolutely nothing like this.

You'll have got home from work later than expected the night before, having struggled to get everything finished on time. You'll need three beers to get you through the Herculean task of packing the clothes, the swimming costumes, the baby paraphernalia and the awkwardly shaped travel cot, and you'll finally get to bed at about 1 a.m., if you're lucky. When the alarm goes off less than four hours later, you'll wake with a mild hangover, made worse by the ironically sobering prospect of a five-hour drive stretching out before you. Having not got round to finishing the packing last night, it'll take you at least an hour to sort that out – and once your kids wake up, it's definitely a case of one step forward, eight steps back, as they excitedly attempt to 'help' you load everything into the car (usually in the rain). What's more, one of you will then feel the need to fulfil the universal yet bizarre desire to vacuum your entire house before you go. What is it about holidays, exactly, that makes us believe we need to return after two weeks to some kind of show home?

At 7 a.m., you are eventually ready to leave, and only then do you realise you forgot to check the oil and tyres. You probably wouldn't have bothered if you were on your own, but your partner asked you to do it and, despite you huffing and insisting everything would be fine, she's having none of it. So off to the petrol station you go, where the children immediately start demanding a snack. Already defeated, you buy a couple of huge bars of chocolate. By the time you're finally on your way, your children are bickering in the back over who deserves another square of Dairy Milk and none of them are showing any signs of sleep (not surprising, really – they've just had ten hours in bed and a huge sugar fix).

At 8.15 a.m., you hit your first traffic jam of the day, and the tedious journey to your destination is inevitably punctuated by regular pit-stops for further snacks, toilet breaks and a grim burger from a service station on the A303. When you arrive at your holiday cottage mid-afternoon, you take a moment to sit in the corner, quietly rocking, as you ask yourself why it was that you were aiming to arrive there so soon. You weren't even meant to have access to the place until 2 p.m., for goodness' sake, so what on earth possessed you to want to get there barely after sunrise?

Last year, for the first time ever, we didn't set off for our summer holiday until around 11 a.m. By that point, all three kids had been up for around five hours, so they were excited but exhausted. This meant they slept in the car for a couple of hours, while my wife and I listened to *our* music for a change, and, when the children woke, we stopped off for lunch at a little café just off the motorway. The remainder of the journey was a little fraught, particularly when the middle one vomited her lunch far and wide, covering not just her siblings but also her parents and much of the luggage, too. But, overall, it was far better than the self-imposed, ridiculously early start of years gone by, which never seemed to benefit anyone.

Holidays with others are great in theory

Just as having kids can show you how different you can be from your closest friends when it comes to parenting, so a holiday with other people (and their kids) can also expose some pretty fundamental differences of opinion that you never knew were there. Holidays with other families are a great idea and, as I should make very clear, they can work brilliantly well. We've been fortunate enough to have some fantastic breaks with close friends of ours, who parent in a similar way and know exactly what makes us and our children tick. But it isn't always that simple.

I once heard of a friendship that had been irrevocably ruined after two families went on holiday together. Unbeknownst to one couple, their friends thought it was perfectly normal to insist on laying the table for breakfast before they all went to bed. The first couple thought this was laughable: surely after the children go down it should be all about sinking into a comfy sofa with a couple of bottles of wine, chatting until the early hours – just like the old days.

Then, whichever poor parent is on duty to get up at the crack of dawn should sit with their bowl of cornflakes watching terrible kids' TV, as they long for their lie-in the next morning. With various children to consider, isn't it ambitious enough to expect everyone to remember to eat breakfast at all, let alone presume it'll be a harmonious affair that's been prepared the night before?

That was just the start. As the week went on, a rising tide of resentment rapidly enveloped these two couples. They both became more entrenched in their views, to the point where failing to pack disposable forks in a picnic bag led to snide remarks about why only one couple could be relied upon to provide for everyone's basic needs. Similarly, when the ultra-organised pair attempted to improve the situation by getting up early one morning to buy eggs, bacon and a mountain of sausages for breakfast, they almost combusted when their friends didn't wake until 9 a.m. – by which point the overcooked sausages had gone completely cold.

Not only did these two couples never go on holiday together again, it was quite some time before they even spoke to each other. Plans for a repeat trip, which had been discussed so much in advance of that first holiday, were never made, and a distance developed that inevitably affected the chances of them remaining close in the future.

One of my friends recently had a similar, albeit less dramatic, experience when on a family holiday: after getting up very early with the children, he spent his entire morning making train tracks, pouring cereal into plastic bowls and watching *Fireman Sam* with only one eye open. This understandably meant he hadn't yet found time to get dressed when the rest of the family suddenly announced it was now time to go for a walk together. Cue much tutting about my friend's lack of organisation, as they waited for him to have a shower – conveniently forgetting that he'd got up about three hours earlier than everyone else to look after the children on his own all morning.

If you're going to go on holiday with friends or family, make sure you think about exactly what you want to get out of your time together. Some people love nothing more than being with every single relative of theirs for the entire time they're away. For me, that's like being slowly suffocated by a feeling of enforced goodwill. I need to occasionally ignore everyone else for a bit, in order to recharge and be ready for some genuine fun en masse a little later. My family understands this; likewise, hopefully I know what defines a good holiday for them. If you haven't first ascertained how all this fits together within your own family setup, you could end up looking forward to your return to work and wondering why on earth you put yourself through the whole experience in the first place.

Washing machines are way more appealing than spa facilities

In the days before children, my wife and I would sit browsing the internet on a Saturday morning, coffee in hand, as we lazily chose the destination for our next holiday. We'd take a close look at the facilities available and, if we could afford it, would plump for places that had an on-site spa, a steam room and a bar with views of the ocean. Now, however, we're far more likely to be tempted by a property with laundry facilities, a cot and a large number of easily-accessible children's TV channels as standard.

My friend Debbie, who is one of four girls, recently told me an unorthodox yet entirely understandable story of her parents' approach to family holidays. Rather than book somewhere overseas at quite considerable cost, they would instead hire a good-value cottage in West Wittering on the south coast of England. The only problem with this otherwise perfect place was that it didn't have a washing machine – something that wasn't exactly ideal with four girls in tow. With the money they saved by not flying any-where, Debbie's parents hired a van in which to transport their washing machine from home to the seaside, and back again, along with all the other luggage. It may seem daft, but if you could only see the pile of suitcases required to take enough clothes for a two-week holiday with four children, you'd surely concur that their approach was actually rather ingenious.

When choosing where to go on holiday with kids, you have to consider their preferences first. If your children are happy, the chances of you also being content are much higher; and yet it's tempting to cling to the idea that hav-ing a family doesn't mean your holidays need to change. Of course, there are plenty of holiday providers who lay on all sorts of wonderful entertainment and activities for children, giving you and your partner a couple of hours to lounge by the pool each afternoon and remember what it was like back in the old days. An experience like that is just a brief moment's pause, though. Generally it's better to look for a place your kids will love, rather than trying to shoehorn in something for them at a destination that isn't at all where they want to go.

One other quick word on this: before you put yourself through the nightmare of a long holiday journey, ask yourself whether it's *really* worth it. If you have children aged two or under, they're never going to remember the supposedly exciting experience of going on an aeroplane. You, however, will have the memory forever etched on your mind, by virtue of the fact that your toddler screamed for the entire duration of the flight. Unless you're visiting family or close friends overseas or heading somewhere you know is going to more than justify the stress of travelling, it's better to spend a few hours in the car than a day and a half schlepping around the world in the name of supposed relaxation.

Your child's definition of 'holiday' is very different from yours

If you're one of those people who used to spend a large amount of your spare cash on going on holiday, it may take a little while to adjust to your child's expectations of a two-week break. You can, of course, continue to fork out thousands of pounds on a luxury fortnight in Mauritius, but it may not be any more meaningful to your children than a cottage by the sea or a holiday park with that slightly dreaded 'entertainment' thrown in for free.

For quite a few years, we were fortunate enough to enjoy a free holiday courtesy of my parents, who let us use their little caravan in Cornwall for our summer break. Having, therefore, saved a small fortune, in the final year before my son started school we decided to treat ourselves to a week out-of-season at Center Parcs in the depths of winter, when it was both relatively cheap and incredibly quiet. We thought our children would instantly appreciate the bike rides, swimming pools, cafés and playgrounds; and, after a day or two, they definitely did. But, for the first 48 hours, my son was primarily suspicious. Surrounded by all this wonderful stuff to do, he simply said: 'Is this *really* a holiday, dad? I don't think it's a proper one. There isn't a caravan here.' For him, contentment on holiday was all about familiarity: he didn't demand an expensive location, unbroken sunshine or access to all sorts of first-class facilities. Instead, holiday happiness was defined as sitting in the van playing snakes and ladders.

In all honesty, it can be quite hard to find a holiday pattern that suits both you and your children. After all, adults very much deserve a break too, and if, in our supposed selflessness, we end up becoming more stressed than we were before going away, no one benefits. It's worth remembering that, in a few short years, your children will no doubt be making it very clear what they expect from a holiday; and, chances are, snakes and ladders in the van will no longer cut it. For the time being, at least, I suggest we rejoice at keeping it simple.

It's a holiday, not a miracle

When your work life is all-consuming, your home life is frantic, and the journeys in between the two are plagued by late-running trains and mile-long traffic jams, it's very tempting to view any forthcoming holiday as the solution to every woe you can possibly think of. Before heading away, you convince yourself that the children will behave beautifully, that the sun will shine throughout and that collectively you will resemble one of those families that travel companies use in their TV advertising, with perfect smiles and impressive physiques. If you invest this amount of expectation in a holiday, the reality is that you're only setting yourself up for failure. Instead of expecting everything to be picture-postcard perfect, try to realistically work out how best to provide the most enjoyable, relaxing break for the entire family. It helps to think things through properly as well: once when we were en route to Cornwall, we stopped off at a supermarket to buy two weeks' worth of food for our holiday. Then we got it back to the car and realised we couldn't actually fit it in alongside all the holiday luggage. My wife and I vowed to never again do the holiday shop until we had arrived at our destination.

Something to be aware of, right from the start, is that holidays can be stressful. When I was aged about twelve, my mum and dad took us to Greece for a couple of weeks. My dad doesn't believe in hanging around, so, despite my mum's protestations, he didn't want to leave a significant amount of time to get to the airport. There was already a dormant layer of tension at this point, which erupted with full force when my then-nine-year-old brother kicked a football through the living-room window. To cut a long story short, the hole was hastily covered up by cardboard and masking tape; not exactly burglar-proof, but there was no time for that. We charged off to Heathrow, arriving with only 15 minutes to spare before the departure gate closed. By the time we were all on board, it certainly took a little while for my parents to embrace fully that archetypal holiday feeling.

It's also smart to avoid the completely unrealistic presumption that your children will behave like angels, purely by virtue of their being away from home. The fact that you've spent a sizeable amount of money on finding somewhere that's just perfect for them doesn't mean they won't bicker, complain or get bored. They're only little, and, if anything, being in an unusual place can make them more likely to misbehave, not less.

Holidays with young children can definitely be more than a little disorienting, not to mention occasionally crazy and stressful. But they are also wonderful, precious, uplifting times, which can act as a real anchor for your family life: a chance to refresh and relax together, as you escape the stresses and strains of the everyday and live at a (slightly) less manic pace for a week or two. Although I've had more than my fair share of holiday moments when the emotions have hit fever pitch, I always come back feeling very strongly reminded of the upsides of being a dad. And much as I find it infuriating at the time, there's even a chance that, one day, I might miss being asked 'Are we nearly there yet?'

Part III

The Bigger Picture

11: Great Expectations

'A two-year-old is kind of like having a
blender, but you don't have a top for it.'

Jerry Seinfeld

As has hopefully been made abundantly clear by now, life
with young children is a largely mad existence, which, due
to the nature of the beast, can mean it's a challenge to think
beyond the here and now. When there's a demanding toddler
clambering all over you and a house that hasn't been dusted
since 1984, when on earth are you meant to find the time
to think about life's bigger issues? It can be hard enough to
tackle the question 'Where are the baby wipes?', let alone
anything along the lines of 'What kind of values do I want to
instil in my children?' But if you never think about the bigger
picture, your existence as a father is reduced to the minutiae
of daily life; whereas, if you take a step back and ponder what
kind of parent you want to be, you should find that the whole
experience is far more fruitful for both you and your children.

In Dad Land, great expectations are there for all to see.
Some are self-imposed; some inherited; and many come
about from the culture that surrounds us. From how much
your kids achieve academically to what a family Christmas
should look like and the amount of money it's appropriate to spend on presents, there's a myriad of hot parenting
potatoes that you need to think about rather than adopt

without question. And it all begins barely a moment after your child is born. I remember being horrified when a dad I knew through work started telling me about the stress of securing a school place for his child. At first, I didn't think there was anything untoward about this – after all, we'd just gone through the rather trying process of confirming our own four-year-old's primary-school place – until I discovered that his daughter was only a month old. Apparently she absolutely had to get into this particular school: the sports facilities were just wonderful and they had an excellent music department, too. This little girl had barely left the womb, yet her education had already been mapped out before her. Having high hopes for your children is a very good thing, but when our expectations for what they will achieve is as ambitious and driven as this, perhaps we need to ask ourselves whether we're in danger of wishing their early years away.

This particular conversation is also relevant when it comes to the thorny issue of money. The dad I was chatting to was a very wealthy man; nothing inherently wrong with that, you might say. But, for many of us, the financial expectations we place on ourselves as parents can cause stress and concern. What, for example, is your definition of a 'treat' going to be, once your children are old enough to appreciate this? Some parents think nothing of taking their kids out to a restaurant after school a couple of times a week; other families simply couldn't afford this. If you have close friends in a very different income bracket to you, you may find that ,when it comes to how you spend money on your children, your definition of normality is very different to theirs.

My dad has an inherent suspicion of coffee shops. We only need to walk past Starbucks for him to declare something along the lines of: 'Skinny this or flat that, paying a stupid amount of money for something they can just make at home – it's bonkers, that is.' And, actually, I think he has a point. As soon as we entered the parenting world, my wife and I joined that rather irritating group of people who are always clogging up cafés with buggies and high chairs, while their children drink horrendously middle-class 'babycinos'. One month, in a desperate attempt to do some proper budgeting, we looked back at how much money we'd spent on taking the kids out for a drink and a snack. Put simply, we could have probably hired our own personal coffee grinder for the same amount. We realised that our two-year-old now expected to be treated to a chocolate twist and some frothy milk whenever we left the house. This is hardly a life-or-death topic, admittedly, but we had allowed his expectation of normality to reach a rather ridiculous level. From that point onwards, trips to the coffee shop became few and far between – and, when we did go, he appreciated the fact that this was something special, which we couldn't afford to do every day.

The topic of money can be a contentious one: in your early twenties, when it came to the question of annual income, you were probably on a fairly level playing field with your contemporaries. People's situations can change very quickly, however, and a decade or two later it can create something of a chasm between you and your mates when discussing what classifies as a reasonable child-related expense. Having kids is financially costly, but there are all sorts of ways of limiting your outgoings without having a negative impact on your family. Freecycle is an amazing resource (any initiative that enables people to give you a piano *and* a Wendy house at no cost gets the thumbs-up from me), as are nearly-new sales, charity shops and hand-me-downs. Conversely, if you're someone who went out regularly before you became a dad, you may find that your outgoings actually decrease once you become a father. In the first year, at least, babies don't need *that* much in the way of food, clothes and toys; now that you're spending your weekday evenings holding a baby bottle instead of a pint, you could discover you end up saving more than you expect.

The question of what to spend – and when – can still catch us out, though. If you're not careful, in your enthusiasm for becoming a dad you'll find yourself purchasing items which may appear essential but which are, in fact, wholly surplus to requirements. As a general rule, I try to avoid anything requiring batteries (I never remember to buy any more of them once they run out) or especially bulky items, which nearly always end up being shoved into a cupboard and will rarely, if ever, appear again. It's often the products that have stood the test of time which are worth spending your hard-earned cash on. Stacking cups, little bricks, tea sets and Lego are all favourites in our household; our kids are happiest when they can let their imaginations run riot, and simple toys are great enablers of exactly that. In a few short years, I'm sure my kids will be pestering me for games consoles, designer clothes and all sorts of yet-to-be-invented products that make the iPad look like something that came in with the Ark; for now, though, I'm enjoying watching them experience the simple pleasures of childhood, which often cost very little in the way of money.

As well as the run-of-the-mill issues that challenge you as a parent, such as how much to spend on toys or leisure activities, it's also crucially important to decide on your expectations when it comes to bigger family events, such as holidays, birthdays and Christmases. Ah, Christmas. The most wonderful time of year. The time when snow is falling, children are playing, and all that. Time for a dose of reality: it never, ever snows in December. As for the children, our most recent Christmas break involved one being sick and another fretting about the fact that he might not remember his lines in the school nativity play. It's supposedly the season for love and understanding; a more accurate description would be the season for being in the office till late, wondering how you're going to get everything finished. And when it comes to 'understanding' within a family, that's easier said than done. I'm still not convinced my gran has forgiven me for failing to pay in the £10 cheque she sent me last June.

Each year, the more Christmas looms, the more I realise my own inadequacies as a parent. Every film, TV programme and advert paints an idyllic picture of family life – but, behind closed doors, there's a baby trying to climb inside the dishwasher, a three-year-old who thinks it would be a great idea to draw a Christmas tree on the kitchen cupboard, and a five-year-old who's seriously worried about whether or not Santa Claus will get stuck in our chimney.

As we approached our first Christmas with three children, my wife and I realised that if we could get to the big day without having some kind of crisis, it would be a miracle on a par with the virgin birth. In a moment of madness, no doubt brought about by a sleepless night, we thought it would be a good idea to host ten adults on Christmas Day. We'd just about got our heads round what we were cooking (answer: turkey, and lots of it) when my dad phoned with a question:

'I've been thinking...', he rather ominously announced. 'Are we having turkey on Christmas Day?'

I confirmed his suspicions.

'Do you think we should have duck as well?'

Clearly not.

'I'd quite like duck.'

That's nice. But you're not having duck. We don't have room in the oven for a duck.

'No problem. Tell you what, I'll just part-cook it at home, then we can finish it off in your oven when we arrive. Everyone else can have turkey, and I'll have my own little plate of duck.'

YOU'RE NOT HAVING DUCK.

On an annual basis, the Christmas-induced stress is exacerbated by the fact that, in my day job, December is the most manic time of the year. There are seemingly endless carol concerts to attend and special programmes to make, all of which results in even less time than usual to write cards or buy presents. One year, we reached the low point of running out of toilet roll. Frankly, I'm not sure how we can be expected to write loving messages to our nearest and dearest when we don't even have the ability to defecate with dignity. After a few Christmases with very young children, we have now decided that we're not going to try to live up to some unachievable festive ideal. You have to swim against the tide, though: all around you, there are magazines with pictures of the perfect Christmas table, and friends can think you're a bit strange when you say you're only going to spend 10 quid on each child because they'll take more pleasure in the wrapping paper than the gift itself.

The arrival of a sibling is a major point at which expectations can be challenged. If you're fortunate enough to have a firstborn who sleeps contentedly through the night and is the very definition of an easy baby, don't be surprised if their little brother or sister takes the polar opposite approach. One of my best mates had a son who was unbelievably contented, easy-going and obedient. For him and his wife, the 'terrible twos' were just a theory; their little boy sailed through his toddler years with nothing more than the occasional whimper when he couldn't find his teddy. His sister, meanwhile, still doesn't sleep well at the age of three, had a double-dose of toddler tantrums to more than make up for her brother's lack of activity in this area, and has been a far more challenging character overall. My friend loves his daughter all the same, of course, but his son's placid nature had completely lulled him into a false sense of security.

In all these areas and a great many more besides, it's so important to talk with your partner about the expectations you both have, not just before you have children but as your children grow up – and about your respective approaches to parenting. I should say here: I'm not presuming everyone exists in a kind of blissful, 2.4 children existence, and

I realise there's a large number of dads in single parent families, perhaps due to the breakup of a relationship, the decision to have a child on their own or the premature death of a partner. But, if you are one of those fathers who is bringing up your children with someone else, you need to be sure that they agree with your decisions way before you move on to trying to get the kids on board. If one of you is, typically, a spender, and the other is a saver, have you discussed how you're going to go about rewarding your child for good behaviour? If you think nothing of purchasing a scooter on impulse, but your other half would consider that to be a present that's only suitable for Christmas and birthdays, you need to talk before you buy.

Once your children reach the age of three, it's a good time to mull over your expectations for how you might be able to involve them in the day-to-day routine of life. Encouraging your toddler to help you in the garden may well result in it taking three times longer than usual to mow the lawn, but the sense of pride they will feel as a result of giving their dad a hand with something important makes such an approach more than worthwhile. Similarly, when baking with your kids, their enthusiasm with the ingredients and their resolute refusal to follow a recipe may not always create the most delicious cakes – but it's the pride they take in making them that's the important thing.

When it comes to great expectations within a family, there's the potentially tricky issue of school, too. When my brothers and I were growing up, there were some boys of a similar age living down the road. My mum invited them and their parents over one evening: we played the board game Scattergories, and I vividly remember how amazed they were that we could win a round against them, given that (as they pointed out rather bluntly) they went to private school and we didn't. Remarks along those lines for the rest of the evening ensured they weren't invited back. It was the first time I realised that not everyone went to the same kind of school as me, and that other people might presume certain things about me by virtue of where I was educated.

Twenty years on and I now find myself considering my own children's education. I'm passionately in favour of the state system and can't imagine ever sending my kids to a private school – and it's for precisely this reason that my wife and I discussed the topic of education before we had children. If you don't take some time to chat through the big questions, you may well find there are a few nasty surprises around the corner when, without warning, you and your partner disagree quite strongly about the direction of travel you should be taking.

Even if you're both confident that you agree on all the big questions of parenting, are you sure your ideas also align with your children's? As your once-tiny baby quickly becomes a confident five-year-old, there's also a danger of foisting your own first loves onto them, regardless of whether or not they actually appreciate this. I was fortunate enough to learn an instrument from a young age and I've gone on to make a career out of my passion for music. As it happens, my wife and I first set eyes on each other in a location that's as about as romantic as a post office: the local school hall, where we played in a concert band together. Consequently, we love the idea of our kids being musical. The middle one definitely seems to be: she's always singing, and telling us she wants to play the trumpet and the drums when she's older. I'm also rather proud that her taste is admirably eclectic: I don't know many three-year-olds who ask to listen to XFM in the car. Our son, meanwhile, hasn't yet shown any real interest in music, but he absolutely loves football. As someone who hasn't progressed further than the toe-punt and who considers himself to have done quite well if he's managed to name a single member of the current England squad, it's clear that my son's love of the beautiful game doesn't come from me. But, as he grows up, I want to make sure I don't push him into playing the cello when he'd be far happier on the terraces or the pitch. And, conversely, if you're a sporty dad who's already looking forward to taking your son to a match every Saturday afternoon, are you willing to adjust your expectations if he doesn't turn out to be as football-mad as you are?

I have very high hopes for all three of my children. I want them to be happy, to succeed in life, to marry brilliant people and to look back on their early years as a time when they were stretched by their parents and encouraged to try out lots of new things. But perhaps, more importantly, I also want them to remember those times when they were allowed to laze about all day without having to get dressed, or develop a love of something completely alien to their parents, or not bother practising their spellings because they were having too much fun playing football in the garden. After all, our children have decades of hard graft ahead of them – so it shouldn't bother us if they haven't saved the world before their teenage years.

12: Pink Versus Blue

'Boys are easy. Like, it's really easy with boys.
It's like, "until you can beat me in a fist fight
you've gotta do what I say!"'

Will Smith

I have two brothers. My dad has two brothers. They both have two sons. My mum is one of four kids and she's the only girl. You get the picture: my family is overwhelmingly male. Growing up, there were never any girls around, bar the occasional obligatory aunt. So, when our first child was born, I wasn't in the least bit surprised that it was a boy. 'It's to be entirely expected,' I thought to myself. 'And if we ever have another, it'll be a boy again – guaranteed.' Then, two-and-a-bit years ago, my first daughter arrived into the world. Suddenly I was presented with the wonderful challenge of being a dad to a little girl. A further surprise came two years after that, when our third child, who I was once again convinced would be a boy, turned out to be nothing of the sort. Being a father to two girls is brilliant: I adore them both (and their brother, for that matter). But, over the last year or so, I've started to worry about what life is going to be like for them growing up.

I vividly remember one particular teatime when my eldest daughter, who was aged just two at the time, declared: 'I not have this cup. It's BLUE.' I'm certainly not one of those parents who insist that their children dress in gender-neutral beige, but, seriously, is it really healthy that a two-year-old girl automatically assumes she can't drink from something because of its colour? And much as I worry about what it will be like for my daughters to grow up in what is still, so often, a world where men get the upper hand, this kind of gender stereotyping doesn't just affect girls. My son unexpectedly burst into tears one morning when I gave him and his sister their breakfast in identical pink bowls (it wasn't a deliberate move; they were the only clean ones to hand, and I couldn't be bothered to empty the dishwasher). What kind of world do we live in where the idea of girls using blue stuff and boys using pink stuff every once in a while is likely to bring children out in a cold sweat?

So-called 'parenting experts' often seem keen to tell us about the differences between boys and girls. I probably shouldn't doubt them – they're the experts, after all – but, from my limited personal experience, I think that, as fathers, we have a real responsibility not to foist society's expectations onto our children, just because of what gender they happen to be. Barely before they've taken their first breath, little girls receive an avalanche of pink clothing, complete with all sorts of fairly nauseating phrases ('Daddy's Little Angel' and the like). Boys, meanwhile, are presumed to love trains, cars and noise, while their sisters sit in the corner benignly stroking cuddly toys. My eldest daughter, currently three, is certainly prone to fairly regular quiet times; but she's equally happy playing with cars and joining in with whatever her older brother happens to be building. It can be even tougher for little boys: discussing this very topic with a few friends recently, one commented: 'Imagine having a son who doesn't like so-called "boy toys". At least girls get to choose and are positively rewarded if they pick toys not marketed at them. Boys are ridiculed if they do the same.'

My experience of bringing up children of both sexes is limited: my eldest girl isn't even four yet, so I don't claim to be an authority here. I do think, though, that as fathers we make quite a strong statement when we choose from the outset to talk about our daughters as our 'princesses', praising them with comments about their physical appearance. I think my two daughters are beautiful, but I'm always very careful to make sure I don't tell them this any more often than I tell my son that he looks great. And as a general rule, it's surely better to sing your child's praises for being kind, helping you out at the shops or trying hard at school, than for looking pretty.

Having said all this, there are clearly some profound differences between girls and boys, and to deny this would be daft. In trying to avoid having your children's identities defined by marketeers of toys, clothes and various other bits of blue and pink tat, there's a danger of going too far the other way, recoiling in horror when your son wants to build a Lego racing car or your daughter desires nothing more than to dress her dolly in bright pink from head to toe. But, in the full knowledge that our young children look to us as their role models, we do need to be making sure we're not shoehorning them into an unhelpful and outdated idea of what it means to be a little boy or girl – especially since this will shape the young person they become in a matter of a few short years.

There is a contrary view, of course. Aren't these worries about the unnecessary 'pink versus blue' divide a little unfounded? Shouldn't we all just relax and let our children conform to a few innocent gender stereotypes, before the full weight of the world descends on their shoulders? My answer is: no, not really. I want all my children to be able to fulfil their potential, and when I see a toy dustpan and brush packaged in a pink box, with the logo *It's a Girl Thing!* emblazoned on the side, as happened in a well-known high-street store not long ago, I feel even more firmly resolved to make sure I don't let my kids be dictated to by people who should know better. Why should my girls be subliminally told that they're best suited to being modern-day Cinderellas, while their brother is encouraged to save the world as Spiderman?

For my youngest daughter's first birthday, we enjoyed a lovely day together, in no small part because she had her head happily buried in cake for most of the afternoon. When our son returned home from school, we opened a few birthday presents, one of which was a JCB-themed bathtime set. It wasn't overtly masculine: there weren't any pictures of men on the box, and nor was it daubed in blue, like many of the toys that are clearly aimed at boys. Nevertheless, my five-year-old instinctively thought that the friends who bought this present for our daughter must have made a mistake. 'That's for me, isn't it?' he enquired. 'My sister can't play with that; I'll have to use it instead.' I like to think we're fairly open-minded as parents and are happy for our kids to play with pretty much any toy they can lay their hands on; but, already, the message that a little construction set could never be right for a girl had permeated my son's mind.

I need to keep a sense of perspective here, I realise: to take that experience as a case in point, it's not as if my son has been brainwashed into inciting violence in the classroom or attacking pensioners on the school run. I also love the fact that my only son is currently happiest when playing football, riding his bike or having a play-fight with me. Success in raising children of different genders is definitely not about getting them to behave in a kind of weird, homogenous way, or in somehow denying the fact that they're male or female. I do, however, think we should step in when we see our children make unhealthy judgments about the world around them. If my son presumes that his sisters can't play with a toy spanner, I need to make sure I double my efforts to broaden his horizons and counteract what our sometimes regressive culture communicates to him.

A further challenge faced by every dad who has a daughter (and by a fair few who have a son, too) is far more pedestrian but no less relevant. It shall for ever be known in our house as the Front Bottom Dilemma. Talking to little boys about their bodies is easy: everything is broadly the same as it is for girls, with the exception of the universally named 'willy'. Everyone knows where they stand with that one. With girls, though, this whole area is a minefield. One of our most bizarre conversations as a couple involved the many different names for female genitalia. I've always found 'front bottom' a little odd: for starters, the phrase suggests it's not as important as the main bottom, and therefore doesn't merit having a name in its own right. Another popular choice, 'fou-fou', sounds like a Japanese martial art or a vegetarian substitute for mince. There's the factually accurate 'vagina' – but it's not exactly a barrel of laughs, that one. I know of a mum who insisted that her daughter should refer to her 'vulva'; anatomically correct, I realise, but I wonder whether this particular parent missed the point a little.

My wife, as it turns out, didn't have a name for that part of her body when she was growing up, but we both agreed we didn't want to take that approach with our three children. As we sat there, debating the merits of various ridiculous words, we realised that coming up with names for our own children was easier than deciding on a term for the female genitals. Later that week, as if by divine intervention, our two-year-old stood up in the bath, covered herself in bubbles from the waist down, and shouted: 'Look! I've got a bubbly noo-noo!' In an instant, our dilemma was solved. The only downside is that this is a name shared by the vacuum cleaner in Teletubbies, which has made for some rather interesting conversation when watching kids' TV.

With all my children, I'm keen to find appropriate ways to demonstrate that they don't need to live up to other people's misguided ideas of what's normal for a little boy or girl. At the same time, it can be hard to do this when so many adults around you appear to want to drive home some kind of 1950s ideal. I was out shopping with all of my kids the other day: hardly revolutionary, but the reaction of the lady at the checkout suggested otherwise. 'Oh!' she exclaimed, with mock astonishment, 'Where on earth is Mummy today?' I was very tempted to reply 'Oh! SHE DIED A TERRIBLE DEATH LAST WEEK,' just to see what kind of reaction I'd get, but I bottled out at the last minute.

It really isn't strange at all for a man to go shopping, any more than it's odd for a little girl to like playing football more than her brother does.

If, like me, you grew up in a very male household, the idea of parenting daughters can be absolutely terrifying. With boys, at every stage I feel like I know where to begin, primarily because of the advantage of having been one myself. Girls, meanwhile, retain an air of mystery. Interestingly, even the dads I know who grew up with sisters around them almost always still profess an instinctive nervousness about what makes their daughters tick. Clearly, no father has experienced what it's like to be a little girl; but, as dads, we're in a unique position to be excellent male role models to our daughters. During their early years, it's highly likely that the number of adult men they look up to will be limited. Nursery staff, playgroup leaders and primary school teachers are overwhelmingly female, making it all the more important that our daughters (as well as our sons) see a good example of male behaviour from us. The tedious stereotype of all dads being beer-swilling, irresponsible and inept doesn't measure up to the reality of most men I know. We want to be good examples to all our children, and every time we enable them to encounter exciting new things, we take a valuable step in that direction.

My first daughter has a very inquisitive mind; she constantly surprises me with her questions, and I'm regularly intrigued by how much she's quietly sussed out about life without her mother or I talking it through with her. I always have to be ready for all sorts of comments that appear from nowhere – and never more so than in relation to the place of boys and girls in the world. Not long ago, we were out for a family walk. As usual, it had taken around seven hours to leave the house, and my wife and I could barely hear ourselves think above the protestations from our eldest two. Already both behaving like teenagers, they were bemoaning how unfair it was that they had to leave the house just when a double bill of *Horrid Henry* was about to start on TV. We ignored their cries of injustice, bundled them into the car with their baby sister and set off into the countryside. Once there, all three children started to enjoy themselves. Out of the blue, as we walked in the bright winter's sun, my daughter looked up to me and said: 'Daddy... when people get married, does the lady's name always become the same as the man's name?' Slightly taken aback, I tried to give an age-appropriate answer without bombarding her with feminist rhetoric, at which point she promptly declared: 'I don't want to not be a Jackson. When I get married to my best friend, my surname is going to be Jackson-Campbell.' In that moment, a little part of me felt very proud, although if she's already that assertive at the age of three, goodness knows what she's going to be like in a decade's time.

The whole 'pink versus blue' issue isn't going to go away any time soon. In fact, I have a feeling that, as my children grow older, it's going to be even more important for me to encourage them to build their own, confident, independent identity, which isn't purely defined by whether or not they have a 'noo-noo' (© my daughter, 2010). I've made a few decisions on this front recently, which I told my wife about. One of them is that I'm definitely not going to 'give my daughters away' if and when either of them gets married.

They're not my possession to hand to another man. And don't give me any of that 'but it's tradition' malarkey. That's not a convincing enough argument. Anyway, there I was, espousing my views in a high-and-mighty fashion. I gave an impassioned speech about why my daughters aren't going to feel pressured into behaving in a particular way when they will, in fact, be headstrong women who stand on their own two feet and are valued for their brains, their compassion and their sense of humour. And then my wife, who's nearly always right, gave me one of those looks before saying: 'When it comes to what happens if and when our daughters walk down the aisle, I'd imagine you'll end up doing whatever they want you to do. After all, they've already got you wrapped around their little fingers.'

13: Tunnel Vision

'My father had a profound influence on me.
He was a lunatic.'

Spike Milligan

Recently, my youngest daughter was awake for three-and-
a-half hours in the middle of the night. I don't mean she
whinged a bit, or wouldn't settle much, or kept drifting in
and out of sleep. Oh no. This was a full-on, 'Come on, Dad,
it's time to blow raspberries on your face', 100 per cent version of awake. In the morning, as her siblings uncoiled like
springs at 6 a.m. and charged into our room, my wife and I
both hid under the duvet in an attempt to ignore the reality
that surrounded us from every angle. Our mumbled conversation centred on both agreeing how much we were looking
forward to life in a few years' time, when we'll once again be
able to get an almost-guaranteed full night's sleep.

Parenting young children is often exhausting, sometimes
infuriating and occasionally quite dull. You slog away in an
attempt do the right thing for your kids, but, when they're
little, they'll often only say thank you if you're bribing them
with a cake, another TV programme or a chance to sit in
the front on the next car journey. (My wife recently had to
travel in the back on a particularly long drive, all because
I'd promised my son the coveted front seat position if he
tried a Brussels sprout. She wasn't happy.) Almost without

realising it, experiences like this can lead you to take a 'tunnel vision' approach to your children, with your eyes firmly fixed on the light that will apparently appear when they're old enough to wipe their own bottoms, fix their own breakfast or get themselves dressed. Friends with older children tell you to 'hang on in there', as if there are sharks circling underneath, ready to snap before you get rescued from the supposed nightmare of having small kids. You remind yourself that, come the teenage years, it'll be you trying to rouse your children from their slumber, not the other way round. And you wistfully imagine what it will be like when, once again, you can finally book a holiday just for the two of you without a travel cot in sight.

Although this is in some ways inevitable, it's also a shame. I think it's vital to revel in the life you have now with your children: I already miss my cute two-year-old son and my tiny baby daughters; they're growing into beautiful little people, but that growth is often too fast for my liking, especially when I realise I spent a large amount of their first few years wishing they knew how to hold a spoon or use a toilet. I now miss the fact that they are no longer as vulnerable as they once were, and although I'm not suggesting for a moment that you should mourn the loss of the potty or shout with joy when you're kept awake all night, I think the aim should be to look for light *within* the tunnel, rather than staying focused on getting through these first few years with the promise of better things to come. For example, we should cherish those moments when our children's naivety shines through; and never more so than when they attempt to tackle life's big questions.

One of the many wonderful things about being the father of small children is the degree to which they see me as some kind of all-conquering, ever-wise hero. I'm very aware that this status I currently hold has a limited shelf-life and that, before long, all three of them will be grunting and sighing at how ineffectual and embarrassing I am. For now, though, I'm basking in the glory of my children seeing me as a wise old sage. There is, however, a fly in the ointment: until they reach the latter stages of primary school, my children genuinely expect me to be able to answer any question they might pose. If you haven't first thought about how you might respond when asked about the meaning of life or the reason why monsters aren't real, you can easily end up being rather flummoxed or, worse still, giving an answer you come to regret.

'I'm really scared, Dad.' So began a conversation with my son one night, when he appeared at our bedroom door long after I thought he had drifted off to sleep. 'When are you going to die?' Before I could attempt some kind of meaningful answer to such a significant question, he immediately followed it up with another thought which, in his mind, was just as important: 'And also, Dad, I'm very sad because when I'm at the really big school, my scooter won't be big enough for me anymore.' I can't really remember my parents' approach to tackling life's big questions with me when I was five, but my attitude is to muddle through and hope for the best. Despite my best intentions, and the fact that I know these questions will definitely come up at some point, things often tend to go awry. I'm still slightly scarred by the whole 'tadpoles' conversation about how babies are made, yet when it comes to the cheery topic of death, it's surely more important to try to give your child a vaguely acceptable answer.

One of the challenges of having school-age kids is that you can no longer sugar-coat everything in life – and nor should you. Our three-year-old still has a blissfully positive and rosy approach: everyone is presumed to be a friend rather than a foe; days are filled with fun activities and play-dates galore; and an awareness of her own mortality has yet to make its mark. But, by the time children are about five, they have an understanding of the world around them and know not everything is always as it should be. So when your child asks you about dying, it's not really acceptable to tell them everything will be okay. Setting kids up with a false sense of security is pretty irresponsible; but, equally, telling them that, actually, Dad could well die tomorrow under a bus or contract some kind of hideous illness isn't exactly the right thing to do either.

I tried to explain a few things to my son: Mum and Dad would hopefully be alive until he's a really big grown-up; if anything ever happens to me, Mum will be here to look after him and his sisters; and there are so many people who love him – grandparents, godparents, friends of ours he delights in playing with – that there wouldn't be any shortage of adults to do the stuff he enjoys doing with Dad. I was actually quite pleased with my answer (it was certainly better than the tadpole one). I felt I'd been clear without overdoing the detail, and I was confident I'd given him a response that even my wife would have been quite impressed with. I waited for a moment, allowing him to take it all in. And then he looked at me, rolled his eyes, and sighed. 'That's fine, Dad – but what about my scooter?'

It may sound obvious, but one oft-forgotten way to avoid tunnel vision when parenting young children is to deliberately foster and encourage their sense of curiosity. I'm the first to admit that it can drive you to distraction when an inquisitive four-year-old asks you 'Why?' for the 24ᵗʰ time in only two minutes, but by fuelling their thirst for knowledge we're surely standing our kids in good stead for the future. Since my early teens, I've enjoyed the fairly heated conversations I have with my dad around the kitchen table. Even today, we roll our eyes when my mum calls out 'Will you two please STOP arguing?', and we respond in unison, 'WE'RE NOT ARGUING; WE'RE CHATTING.' He's always encouraged my brothers and me to grapple with life and never just accept the status quo, and I know that his refusal to simply respond 'Because I said so' in answer to our numerous questions has had a positive effect on me. I now need to constantly remind myself to do the same thing with my own children.

My three year old is a particularly curious child: I've recently had to answer everything from 'Why don't we have the same bedtime?' to 'Is your grandpa still dead?' She asks all sorts of questions, from the mundane to the profound; and when I'm trying to leave the house, already running five minutes late, I rarely appreciate being asked 'Where's my bunny gone?' or 'Do cats go to heaven?' I often have to stop myself from letting on that her questioning is a little tiresome: after all, if she grows up thinking that her dad was only happy when she didn't ask him anything, it doesn't bode well for our communication once she's a teenager. My daughter's probing approach to life makes her who she is, and, as her father, it's definitely not my job to stifle that. I've frequently fallen into the trap of being so keen to look ahead to when my children are older that I've inadvertently wished away the present moment. And if you're anything like me, you'll find yourself being particularly prone to this approach when you're tired, irritated or have had a day at work that you would rather forget.

My walk home from the local railway station takes exactly four minutes, and those four minutes are often the most important time of the day. My hour-long commute will nearly always involve wading through an inbox of emails (on an average day, 50 per cent are along the lines of 'Has anyone seen my pen?', 30 per cent are press releases written by people whose spelling is so bad it's a wonder they know how to write their own name, and 20 per cent are actually relevant to what I do for a living). If my working day has been a challenge, it's so easy to let the stress overshadow my arrival home, too. On my little walk, I have to consciously park the stuff that's filling my mind and instead remind myself that for the next twenty minutes, the three bouncing beans I'm about to encounter as I walk through the door are my number one priority. On the occasions when I don't take a moment to reflect and let go of the stresses and strains of the day, I find myself wanting to get the kids to bed quickly. They become another task to be accomplished, rather than being the people who I'm there to encourage, uplift and enjoy the company of before they drift off to sleep. Although it can feel a little contrived at times, making a deliberate decision to let go of the baggage of work and ensure your children are your sole focus is a very liberating experience.

It's not only at bedtime that we need to ensure we're ready to listen to what our kids have to say. When it comes to the questions they pose, you can be fairly certain that, at some point before their fifth birthday, they will have touched on topics like where babies come from, the reason people die or why it's not fair that they can't get a goldfish. One of the joys about young kids, though, is how unpredictable their comments can be. I tell myself I've got it sussed as a parent; and then, out of nowhere, something so bizarre appears I end up wondering whether my wife put something hallucinogenic in the coffee.

A few weeks ago, I had mild cause for concern when it came to the subject of my son's education – and the associated views he had formed as a result. Flicking through what was on television on Sunday afternoon, I came across *The Magnificent Seven*: a sure-fire hit for a five-year-old boy. He gleefully watched the cowboys onscreen and, a moment later, some rather evil-looking men appeared, brandishing guns.

'I know who *they* are, Dad,' my son confidently declared.

I let him explain…

'THEY are the Catholics.'

I was sure I must have misheard him. Nope…

'The Catholics, Dad. They've got guns.'

What *had* his teachers been telling him? I needed to know more about this display of unfounded intolerance. Tempted as I was to call his mum into the room for the rest of this conversation, I thought I should bite the bullet (if you'll pardon the pun).

'That's interesting. Why do you think they're Catholics?'

'Because they've got guns and they're going to kill the king.'

After some further gentle questioning, it transpired that his class had been learning about the Gunpowder Plot at school. The men on the screen had guns. Therefore they must be Catholics. End of story. Life really is wonderfully simple when you're only five. We talked about cowboys for a bit, and about Catholics for a little longer. My boy now knows they're not necessarily one and the same. The lady he spends six hours a day with every weekday is not, on closer examination, teaching him anything fundamentally bigoted – which is a relief, because our allotted time with her at parents' evening just isn't long enough to allow for a discussion of our son's spelling test *and* her views on inciting religious hatred.

The main reason why we have a family quotes book on our kitchen shelf is so that we can remember these mad yet uplifting pronouncements from our children. When you're caught up in the everyday moments, your focus as a parent is on trying to get out of the house on time or attempting to cook breakfast without your toddler grilling her hand. There isn't always time to lightheartedly reflect on the quirky comment made by your angelic child (not when they're busy pulling their sibling's hair, anyway). After a particularly trying day, once the children are in bed, I'll often sit down, flick through the book and head back into the mad parenting tunnel for a moment. As I read comments like 'Mum... do bananas have willies?' or 'Daddy, are you a man or a lady?' (a particularly worrying question, given that it was posed while I was sharing a bath with my then-two-year-old son), I happily reflect on the immense privilege it is to be a dad to these three children. At the time these comments were made, chances are we were stressed, late, tired or a combination of all three; after the event, I can see the bigger picture – and rather beautiful it is too.

Nevertheless, it's undoubtedly true we *do* need to frequently remind ourselves that life won't always be this chaotic. There's nothing wrong with that; if we didn't, we'd probably weep. My cousin recently had an especially sobering experience in this respect, which understandably led her to look forward to her son being a little older. Her little boy was playing happily in the kitchen when, all of a sudden, he was inexplicably sick all over the floor. At the moment she went to clear it up, the dog then walked in with an almost-dead mole in between his teeth. It deposited the animal at her feet, adding some of its own vomit, and stood there for a moment. My cousin's little boy then did an exploding poo, which started to seep out of his nappy. As his mum surveyed the situation and tried to summon up the strength to start clearing up the appalling mess, the overpowering sights and smells led to her also being sick. In that moment, it would be fair to say she didn't want to remain in the tunnel any longer. Instead she needed someone to rescue her from it and transport her away as far as possible – preferably with a bottle of Febreze and a large glass of Rioja.

The challenge is to try to strike a balance between on the one hand reminding ourselves that the madness will one day subside, and on the other enjoying the craziness of the moment. Once your children start school, some of the best years of their lives are already behind them. This isn't meant in a doom-laden way; it's merely an acknowledgement that being four years old is undoubtedly awesome. It can be so tempting to see children's early years as a time you have to 'get through', as if the Promised Parenting Land on the other side will make all that toil worthwhile. Instead, maybe we need to embrace the chaos, the ridiculous questions and the vomit (well, maybe not the vomit) and really enjoy what our kids have to offer at this very special time. And then, when we look back on those years from a distance, we can be confident that we gave them the best possible springboard into the rest of their life, even if our memory of the early years whirlwind is decidedly out-of-focus.

14: We Are Family

'The guys who fear becoming fathers don't understand that fathering is not something perfect men do, but something that perfects the man. The end product of child-raising is not the child but the parent.'

Frank Pittman

Six years ago, my wife and I sat in our tiny, one-bedroomed flat, nervously discussing the arrival of our first child in a few months' time. As the world of parenting loomed, we felt a mixture of awe, excitement and absolute terror. Fast forward on to today, and we've muddled through to the point where our family now feels complete. (Apologies in advance if you're my fourth child and you're reading this; yes, you evidently weren't planned. But we love you all the same.) As we begin to emerge from the chaos of those early years, and the rest of their childhood looms into view, what do I want my family life to look like for the next couple of decades? Whether you have a houseful of children or just the one baby, it's helpful to think about what you want your family identity to be. And it all starts by rewinding the clock back to your own upbringing.

One of the many things I love about my dad is how gloriously anti-social he can be. The contrast between him and my mum couldn't be stronger: she'll chat to absolutely anyone, regardless of whether or not they're in any way interested in what she has to say; my dad, meanwhile, rejoices in his hermit-like status and will happily let several days pass without having spoken to anyone except the dogs. As a little boy I cherished our Saturdays as a family, largely because of the way in which my dad prioritised our time together above anything with other people. He would frequently declare over breakfast that this time of the week was for just the five of us. The regular pattern of Saturday morning activities (swimming at the local pool, followed by a doughnut and a cheese straw afterwards) created a sense of equilibrium and regularity, which my brothers and I all appreciated. Even in our teenage years, we would try to keep Saturday mornings clear, despite the fact that they no longer involved a swim and a doughnut.

As someone who's naturally more sociable than his father (after cutting my hair, a barber once told me I could 'talk for Britain'), I'd like to feel I've inherited that same sense of protection over our time as a family of five, even if I might be more inclined to pack in plenty of other events as well. When my kids look back on their childhood, I want them to remember with fondness the fact that we didn't always accept invitations to every social occasion or extended family gathering. Occasionally, and with young kids especially, we need to refuse to answer the phone and enjoy not having to interact with anyone other than our immediate family.

The question of how much to try to replicate your own childhood can be a sobering one, though, especially since it raises that rather terrifying question of whether or not we eventually become our parents. One of the things I love the most about staying with my mum and dad is their willingness to get up with the children at the crack of dawn. On New Year's Day, there is nothing sweeter than being able to say to two under-fives when they appear at your bedside: 'Go and see Grandad. Goodbye.' What's more, the fact that my dad doesn't come into our room at 8 a.m. and consider that to be enough of a lie-in, purely because he's been up with the kids for a couple of hours by this point, is something for which I'll always be thankful. If and when I have grandchildren (a ridiculous thought, I know, given that I sometimes wonder how it's even possible for me to have kids of my own already), I hope I'll show the same consideration to my brood and happily rise in the early hours to watch the 2040 equivalent of *Abney and Teal*.

Whenever I've spent a meaningful amount of time with my parents, the idea that I'll one day be just like my dad fills me with a bizarre mixture of serene contentment and what can only be described as paralysing fear. Although I love his considerate nature and his eagerness to ensure that my wife and I relax whenever we stay at my parents' house, there remain some things that deeply panic me about the prospect of becoming more and more like him. Don't get me wrong: I wouldn't have him any other way and he is, of course, the best father anyone could ever have, but it's surely okay to have at least a few quibbles, isn't it?

His ability to get his words confused, for example, isn't something I want to emulate in a hurry. When planning dinner recently, he announced to the assembled throng that we'd be having 'a lesbian meal – all together'. Just your average evening in the Home Counties, then. (Upon further enquiry, he grudgingly admitted that he had, in fact, meant 'Lebanese' – but it's an easy mistake to make. We've all been there.) His choice of attire is never less than interesting, either. My dad remains the only man in the world who believes it to be entirely normal to wear a large green bum bag at the supermarket ('Why would anyone want to have to reach into their pocket for a wallet when you can access your money via one easy zip?'), and he resolutely refuses to remove his jumper when eating, even if he's practically dying from the heat ('I just don't believe in taking my pullover off at the table – and anyway, it wouldn't make me any cooler; it simply doesn't work like that').

A couple of months ago, before we left his house to head home, I mentioned to my dad that I was writing a book about parenting. 'You? Parenting? What on EARTH do YOU know about parenting?' It's a fair response – but then, the beauty of finding your way as a dad is that none of us has a clue how to do it. We're all attempting to keep calm, carry on and do our best; which is a relief, really, because if it required anything more than that, I doubt any man would qualify for the task.

Decisions you make about what you want your family to look like can often be shaped by both positive and negative experiences of your own childhood. To a large extent, you can choose what to emulate and what to disregard – but there are many aspects of life as a father that aren't so easy to control. For example, a major moment that can often redefine the identity of a family is the arrival of a sibling. Many people choose not to have a second child; there are

also couples who would desperately like their son or daughter to have a sibling, but cannot conceive again. I wouldn't for a moment want to suggest that a family with an only child is in any way incomplete; however, with over half of UK families containing two or more children, it's inevitable that a great many of us will face the enjoyable task of parenting more than one little person, whose relationship with their brother or sister is entirely independent of their relationship with us.

When our first daughter was born, my wife and I thought we had it all sussed. We'd done the whole baby thing before and we therefore reckoned it would all be relatively simple – certainly more than simple than the first time round. How wrong we were. When our second child arrived, we realised how much time we had on our hands when we only had one baby to consider. When they slept, we slept; now, while our new baby slept, the toddler expected to be entertained with boundless energy and enthusiasm. There's also the whole issue of sibling rivalry to contend with. Even the most easy-going of two-year-olds will have their patience tried by a baby who throws their toy across the room or lands a perfectly placed spoonful of yoghurt on their face. Although I frequently fail in this area, I want my family identity to include space for my kids to develop their own relationship with each other, without my wife or me forever getting in the way. When your children start to bicker, it's so tempting to step in and resolve the situation. Clearly, if one of them is in danger of losing a limb, it's probably time to intervene, but, as a general rule, it's better to let your kids try to come to a resolution without you always having to be the arbiter of who's right or wrong.

A further challenge with the arrival of more children relates to whether or not you view your kids equally. Before the birth of my daughters, I genuinely worried about whether or not I would love them as much as I loved my son. His arrival into the world was so awesome, life-changing and emotional, and it was followed by seeing him spend two years growing into a beautiful little boy. Deep down, much as I wanted him to have a brother or sister, I shared the secret concern of many parents in thinking that I might not be so enthusiastic about our new arrival. And yet, within a moment of holding my first daughter, any such feelings immediately dissipated – something that also happened when my second daughter made her very speedy entrance into the world.

There are many things that get the thumbs up when it comes to growing up as the eldest child in a fairly large family. As the first of three boys, I was lucky enough to always get clothes from a shop rather than a sibling, to be the one to try out all sorts of new experiences, and to embrace pretty much every rite of passage before my brothers. There were some down sides, too, though: as I mentioned earlier, I've never understood quite why my mum felt the need to keep my umbilical cord in a childhood photo album. It was only thrown away about three years ago, and I was lucky enough to witness the ceremonial disposing of what looked like a piece of small gristle nestled in between pictures of me in my cot. My mum apart, I don't think any of us mourned the loss of that particular part of my/her anatomy from the family archives, and nor do I feel its continued presence up to that time will go down as a particular highlight for me when it comes to the benefits of being the firstborn.

Having said that, I suppose it's quite nice that my mum kept such a comprehensive record of my first few months. I'm not sure my brothers can look back on such a detailed account of their early years. In fact, by the time the youngest one came along, he was lucky to have any photos taken of him before the age of about five, let alone enjoy a chunk of his cord being preserved. The middle one and I have often tried to convince the youngest – known to us all as 'the runt of the litter' – that this lack of attention stems from the fact that my parents love him much less than they do us. 'You do know you were meant to be a girl, don't you?' remains a favourite taunt to this day (only ever in jest, you realise). I don't *think* it's left him with permanent scars.

As a father, I've now personally discovered how difficult it can be to give all your children the same level of attention, especially in those first few weeks after their arrival into the world. My youngest daughter is barely over a year old, and I'm acutely aware that she's already being slightly overlooked in some ways. She just seems to have slotted in to life as the youngest one already, and has no option but to go with the Jackson flow. A couple of months after her birth, I parked the car in Tesco and wandered off to do the shopping, only to be reminded by my wife that it might be a good idea to get the baby out of the car. I'd completely forgotten she was there; after all, compared to her brother and sister at that age, she was a very easy child who didn't feel the need to make her presence known every couple of minutes. I hadn't even bothered to park in the Parent and Child space, because I genuinely thought I couldn't justify it without the children; a little later in the day, when booking a holiday on the phone, I panicked when asked what my youngest daughter's date of birth was, quickly realising that 'January, when it was quite icy' wasn't specific enough. The fact that, by contrast, I could recite not just my eldest's date of birth but the precise time, too, made me feel more than a little guilty.

I recently read a quote from a parent who seemed to sum all this up perfectly: 'When I had my first child he had his own face cloth. My second child shared his brother's face cloth. And my youngest had the dish cloth.' In our house, no one has a face cloth – we have been known to tell them to wipe their face on their T-shirt because we can't be bothered to find a flannel. But when it comes to our family identity, I often think I should do a little more to make sure that Child Number 3 gets as much focus and attention as Child Number 1. For what it's worth, my advice to anyone with more than one child is to think back to what you did with your firstborn during their early years, and ask yourself whether you're investing the same amount of time in your second, third or fourth arrival (based on my frantic experiences so far, anyone who has more than four children is clearly cither clinically insane or is a member of some kind of sect). If we want all our kids to have happy memories of their early years, we need to make sure they feel equally loved.

Almost from the moment you arrive home from the hospital with your newborn baby, you will start to face questions about your child's development. I find much of this to be very tedious: when people ask me how old my kids were when they started walking, I've no idea what to say, mainly because it never really bothered me. I knew my children would walk eventually, and that I wouldn't still be needing to push them around in a buggy by the time they reached school-age – so why should I remember the precise moment of their first steps? There are numerous other milestones (first solid food, first crawl, first poo in the potty) which, let's face it, are never going to set the world alight. But if you share my slightly dismissive attitude about remembering moments such as these, it's important not to negate your responsibilities towards those areas of your child's development that you *can* influence. Playing games with kids from a young age encourages them to socialise, share and interact with the people around them; reading stories at bedtime engenders a sense of routine at the end of the day, and also plays a central role in their understanding of language; and encouraging them to try different foods as soon as they've progressed beyond the milk stage increases the likelihood of them having a more adventurous palette during the toddler years and beyond. The more unadulterated time you are able to spend with your child, the better their chances of interacting happily with all sorts of other people, from kids the same age at the local playgroup through to relatives many decades older than them.

When you strip it away to its absolute core, the essence of fatherhood is all about preparing to let your children go. The other day, my five-year-old son got very tearful when I suggested he might not live with us forever; in his world, next week is a lifetime away, and his early twenties are unimaginable. I suspect, however, that once his teenage years are drawing to a close, even he will relish the opportunity to start making a life for himself somewhere else. Everything we do as dads ultimately focuses on preparing our children for a world in which we are involved in their daily lives to a much lesser extent than we are now, and that's something that is hard to take on board at times.

Sigmund Freud once famously commented: 'I cannot think of any need in childhood as strong as the need for a father's protection.' That quote was first published in 1930, which may lead you to assume it's out of date. After all, hasn't the world of fatherhood moved on since those days? In many ways, life as a father in the 21st century is very different to the experiences of those who were bringing up children nearly 100 years ago: back then, phrases like 'paternity leave' and 'stay-at-home dad' were a long way from conception. My very limited experience of parenting spans just over five years; I know there will be all sorts of challenges ahead as my children power on towards their teenage years and beyond. Nevertheless, it's already clear to me that the protection we give our children by helping them feel secure in their family is one of life's greatest privileges. What's more, although we might think that parenting involves ensuring our children learn about the world around them, it's equally about gaining an understanding of who we are and what we're capable of as fathers.

So far my experience has encompassed a catalogue of errors, with plenty of examples that would ensure failure at the first hurdle of any official parenting test. Despite all this, over the last five years my kids and I have had a riot. You're never ready for fatherhood; if you had to be, the human race would quickly die out. It's messy, it's exhausting and, for many years, you often feel like you don't have a clue what you're doing. Despite all this, fatherhood is the most amazing journey you could ever hope to embark upon. And, amid the chaos, the sleepless nights and the countless mistakes, being called 'Dad' remains the most wonderful experience in the world.

Acknowledgements

A couple of years ago, I rambled away to Olivia Bays from Elliott & Thompson about how I'd love to one day write this book. Without her enthusiasm, honest feedback and good humour, it would have remained a pipe-dream; the fact that it's actually happened is very much down to Olivia, and I therefore owe her an enormous debt of gratitude. The support of the rest of the team at E&T has also been invaluable: Lorne, Pippa, Jennie, Alison and Thomas, thank you so much for believing in my idea, taking my words and turning them into something much more special.

My boss, Richard Park, has been hugely supportive throughout, and I'm very grateful to him for this. I'd also like to express my gratitude to Darren Henley, Managing Director of Classic FM, for giving me the opportunity to author books in the first place. His continual encouragement and wisdom as I've branched out into writing about something firmly outside my classical music comfort zone is massively appreciated. Finally, I couldn't be the dad I am without the constant love and support of my wife and best friend. Helen: I'm still a little confused as to why you thought I would be a suitable father for your children, but I'm having great fun on this parenting journey with you. Also, sorry for including the story about 'the trim' when I said I wouldn't. I hope you don't mind.

Biography

Sam Jackson is a writer, blogger, and Managing Editor of national radio station Classic FM – a role he has held since 2011.

In February 2014, Sam was named as one of the Evening Standard's 20 best bloggers for his popular blog Diary of a Desperate Dad. His account of living with three young children, which inspired this book, was described by the Evening Standard as 'a must for veteran parents or those new to the game'. In 2013, the Hospital Club named Sam one of 'the 100 most influential, innovative and interesting individuals in the media and creative industries', and in 2012 he was listed in the Music Week *30 Under 30*.

In addition to writing about fatherhood, Sam has co-authored four books about classical music: *The Classic FM Hall of Fame, Everything You Ever Wanted to Know About Classical Music...But Were Too Afraid to Ask, 50 Moments That Rocked the Classical Music World,* and *The Big Book of Classic FM* (all published by Elliott & Thompson). A proficient pianist and clarinettist, Sam sits on the governing body of Trinity Laban Conservatoire of Music and Dance, and his work has been honoured by the Radio Academy Awards, the New York International Radio Festival and the Arqiva Commercial Radio Awards.

Prior to writing about parenting, Sam's decade in the radio industry included five happy years behind the microphone as a presenter on children's radio station FUN Kids. Today, you can find him on Twitter @classicjacko.

Resources

One thing you very quickly realise when you become a dad is that pretty much everyone you've ever met is more than willing to give you parenting advice. Some of that advice is helpful, of course, but an awful lot of it is rather questionable, so I've found it really helpful to use a few trusted resources that are packed full of tips, tricks and words of wisdom. The books and websites below are all good places to turn for advice, encouragement or a different perspective on parenting. I hope you find them as useful and relevant as I have.

The Parenting Book by **Nicky and Sila Lee** (Alpha International, 2009)
Nicky and Sila Lee have decades of experience in mentoring and counselling parents, and their book is, quite simply, the finest parenting book around. Married for over 30 years and with four grown-up children themselves, they are very well-placed to talk about the highs and lows of family life, and they do so with very impressive honesty. Off the back of the book's success, Nicky and Sila also developed The Parenting Course. Although written from a Christian perspective, the

book and the course are relevant to parents of any faith and none. I've frequently turned to *The Parenting Book* when times have been a little tough.

It's Not Raining, Daddy, It's Happy by Benjamin Brooks-Dutton (Hodder & Stoughton, 2014)
Of all the blogging dads online, Benjamin Brooks-Dutton is by far the most inspirational. His story is tragic: he was widowed at the age of 33, when his son was aged just two. Shortly afterwards, he began his blog, Life as a Widower. The raw emotion and very real challenges of being a single parent, coupled with humour and tenderness, make it a must-read. Benjamin's new book, *It's Not Raining, Daddy, It's Happy*, tackles fatherhood, grief, and love, and provides powerful proof that there's no 'one size fits all' family, highlighting the different challenges of individual circumstances.

The Fatherhood Institute (www.fatherhoodinstitute.org)
The Fatherhood Institute describes itself as being 'The UK's fatherhood think-and-do tank'. Their website is a really useful resource for the latest research on the effect fathers have on their children's upbringing; the vision of the Institute is of 'a society that gives all children a strong and positive relationship with their father and any father-figures; supports both mothers and fathers as earners and carers and prepares boys and girls for a future shared role in caring for children'.

Mumsnet (www.mumsnet.co.uk)
It's a potentially scary world, is Mumsnet. As you infiltrate their pages, you feel like the only dad in the playground at

If you enjoyed reading this book, visit Sam's blog at diaryofadesperatedad.com for more accounts of his parenting adventures.

school pick-up time, overhearing various women in conversation about everything from tips to get their child to sleep through to how much sex it's normal to be having after the birth of a baby. Despite the obvious female focus of the site, it's actually full of resources for parents of both sexes. There are book reviews, blog recommendations and seemingly endless discussion topics, which range from the eminently useful to the frankly bizarre. For ample proof of the latter, search online for 'Mumsnet penis beaker'…

Telegraph Men

If you need convincing that there's more to the 21st century man than beer, boobs and football, follow @TelegraphMen on Twitter. This rapidly growing section of the Telegraph's website is home to all sorts of diverse articles about the place of men in Britain today. What's more, there are regular features on parenting from @CommandoDad, who provides an amusing and practical take on fatherhood.

Parentdish.co.uk

This vibrant website is a rich resource for finding out the latest news about parenting. Their homepage offers 'News, views and advice for parents', which can mean anything from an article about 'Dad bragging' (why are modern-day fathers so intent on boring everyone with stories about their children?) through to '10 maternity wear essentials' (not necessarily that relevant for dads – but certainly useful if you need to buy your pregnant partner a birthday present). The site is regularly updated with articles and features, and is as relevant to us men as it is to our other halves.